HE SECRETS OF THE CHRISTMAS

Dark Supernatural Christmas Mystery of Haunted Books, Hidden
rses, and the Search for Redemption

- SUSAN ABRAHAM

Published by *Koppiha Pathfinders*

ISBN: 9798301064029

Cover Design: Kaimor Dee'signs

Re-Editing: Jim Dick

Dedication

To my mother, Mrs. Eno Nse, whose unwavering support has made this journey possible.

Preface

"There is no greater treasure than a book—until you find the one that should have never been opened."

Amidst the cobbled streets of historic Dublin stands a bookshop unlike any other. Its name has been forgotten by many, its dusty windows offering no sign of life, yet the curious are always drawn to it. Some are captivated by its shelves overflowing with ancient, leather-bound volumes. Others feel an inexplicable pull, as though summoned by the building itself.

Few know the truth about this place: it holds secrets far darker than the faded ink of its books. Generations of keepers have come and gone, each bound by a curse older than the city itself. To inherit the bookshop is to inherit its shadows, its whispers, and the terrible price it demands.

Daniella never intended to step into this world of hidden curses and forbidden knowledge. She was just another woman lost in the aftermath of failure, looking for a way to survive. But the bookshop doesn't choose its keepers lightly, and now she stands at the crossroads of salvation and destruction.

This is a story of love and loss, of betrayal and redemption, of choices that carve paths through destiny. And above all, it is a story

*secrets—those buried in the pages of books, and those that haunt
e hearts of the living.*

*the snow falls this Christmas, the shop's newest keeper will learn
e truth: not all gifts are blessings, and not all stories have happy
dings.*

rs. Anita Anderson, PhD

Title Page 1

Copyright 2

Dedication 3

Preface 4

Prologue 7

TABLE OF CONTENTS

Chapter 1: *Shattered Reflections* 9

Chapter 2: *The Bookshop of whispers* 16

Chapter 3: *Echoes in the Dark* 23

Chapter 4: *The Price of Knowledge* 38

Chapter 5: *Beneath the Surface* 51

Chapter 6: *The Unraveling* 63

Chapter 7: *The Broken Bridge* 77

Chapter 8: *The Echo of Choices* 86

Epilogue 99

PROLOGUE

ome secrets were never meant to be uncovered, yet they wait—
tient, persistent, and powerful—until the right soul dares to turn
e page."

he bookshop sat at the end of a narrow, cobbled street, shrouded in
e perpetual twilight of its ancient windows. A thin layer of frost
ng to the glass, though the air outside had been unseasonably
arm for days. Inside, time seemed to stall; the ticking of the
tique clock on the counter was the only sound breaking the
ence.
the shadows of the back room, a man sat at an oak desk, his head
nt over an open book. His trembling fingers traced the words
ched into the yellowed parchment, words that seemed to shift and
rithe under his gaze. The faint glow of the single candle beside
m illuminated his face—worn, hollow, and etched with
speration.
t must be done," he whispered to himself, his voice cracking under
e weight of fear.
he book responded. Its words swirled together into a vortex of dark
k, forming symbols he couldn't decipher. A low hum filled the
om, resonating deep in his chest like the toll of a distant bell. He

leaned back, clutching his chest as the hum grew louder, reverberating through the walls of the bookshop.

The candle flickered violently before extinguishing altogether. The darkness that followed was thick, almost alive, wrapping itself around him like a suffocating cloak.

The man gasped, reaching for the book, but it slammed shut with a force that rattled the desk. A chill wind swept through the room, carrying with it the faint sound of whispers.

"You have failed," the voices hissed in unison, echoing from every corner of the shop.

"No!" he cried, clutching at the book. "Please, give me more time!" But the bookshop had no mercy. The hum became a roar, and the man's scream was swallowed by the shadows.

When the morning sun finally pierced the frost-covered windows, the shop was quiet once more. The desk sat empty, save for the closed book resting at its center. Its cover, black as midnight, bore no title, only the faint imprint of a hand—proof of the man who had dared to defy it.

Out in the bustling streets of Dublin, life continued unaware of the dark force that had claimed another soul. But the bookshop remained, waiting. It always waited—for the next keeper, the next fool, the next chapter to be written.

And somewhere, not far away, a woman named Daniella was about to step into its shadows, her fate already sealed by secrets she didn't yet know existed.

Chapter One: SHATTERED REFLECTIONS

Sometimes, life shatters your plans to guide you toward the path you were truly meant to follow."

Daniella stared at the tattered termination letter in her trembling hands, the black ink smudged by her tears. She sat on the edge of her bed in the tiny apartment she could no longer afford, her suitcase lying open on the floor, a silent reminder of how quickly life can unravel.

Two weeks before Christmas. Fired. The department store she'd poured years into no longer saw her as valuable. She had given her all to that place—overtime, late shifts, even sacrificing holidays—but in the end, it hadn't mattered. Loyalty, it seemed, was just another empty word.

Her phone buzzed besides her, cutting through the heavy silence. It was her mother. Have you spoken to Maria? Spend Christmas with her this year. She wants you there.

Daniella rolled her eyes. Maria wanted her there? Doubtful. Maria was the golden child, the picture-perfect sister with the picture-perfect family. Daniella could already imagine the forced smiles and subtle jabs hidden behind a facade of holiday cheer. Still, what choice did she have? Staying here, in the suffocating quiet of her apartment, wasn't an option.

She tossed the letter onto the suitcase and stood. The faint glow of Christmas lights from her window painted the room in streaks of red and green, mocking her with their cheerfulness.

The train to Dublin was cold and crowded, the holiday rush evident in the weary faces of fellow passengers. Daniella watched the world blur past the frosty window, her reflection barely visible. Her mind churned with dread over what awaited her.

Maria's home was immaculate, as expected. Daniella walked into a pristine hallway, the scent of cinnamon and pine filling the air. Maria greeted her with a polite hug that lacked warmth. Her nieces and nephews peeked at her from behind the bannister, curious but cautious.

"Glad you could make it," Maria said, her tone as rehearsed as her perfectly curled hair.

"Did I have a choice?" Daniella replied, shrugging off her coat.

Maria's lips tightened, but she said nothing, leading Daniella into the living room where their mother sat, beaming.

"I'm so happy you're here!" their mother exclaimed, pulling Daniella into a genuine hug.

Daniella smiled faintly, trying to suppress the bitterness brewing inside her. She wanted to snap, to tell her mother that Maria didn't want her here, that she was just a seasonal charity case. But she bit her tongue, for now.

aniella smiled faintly, trying to suppress the bitterness brewing
side her. She wanted to snap, to tell her mother that Maria didn't
ant her here, that she was just a seasonal charity case. But she bit
r tongue, for now.

was during dinner that her mother brought up the bookshop.
Daniella, I have a friend in need of help. He owns a charming
ookshop in the city, but it's struggling. You're so good with
ganizing things. I thought you might lend a hand while you're
re."

aniella nearly choked on her wine. "A bookshop? You want me to
ork over Christmas?"

t's not a job, dear. Just a little help. Mr. Peters is a kind man, but
's… getting on in years. The shop could use someone like you."

aria chimed in, her voice dripping with forced encouragement. "It
ight do you some good. Keeps you busy, right?"

aniella glared at her sister but said nothing. In truth, it wasn't like
e had anything better to do.

ine," she muttered. "I'll do it."

er mother beamed, Maria smirked, and Daniella silently cursed
rself for agreeing. Little did she know, stepping into that
ookshop would unravel far more than dusty shelves and forgotten
mes—it would unravel her very life.

aniella woke to the faint sounds of children's laughter and the
oma of freshly baked bread wafting through Maria's house. The
orning sunlight spilled into the guest room, illuminating the stark

contrast between her chaotic inner world and Maria's flawlessly curated life.

She dragged herself out of bed, not because she wanted to but because staying under the covers wouldn't shield her from the day ahead. After all, she had agreed to this—though now, the idea of playing the role of a helpful sister was as appealing as eating glass. Maria was in the kitchen, humming as she whisked batter with an energy that made Daniella's tired bones ache. The twins, Jack and Ava, were bickering over who got the last pancake while the youngest, Lily, sat quietly coloring at the table.

"Oh, good. You're up," Maria said without looking up from her task. "Breakfast is almost ready. Coffee's over there."

"Morning to you, too," Daniella muttered, pouring herself a cup. Their mother bustled into the room, already dressed as though she had an important social engagement. "Daniella, darling, we'll be going to the bookshop today to meet Mr. Peters. I think you'll love it—such charm, so much history!"

Daniella bit back a groan. The last thing she wanted was to spend her morning in a dusty old shop, but there was no point arguing.

"Great," she said flatly, taking a gulp of coffee.

Maria finally glanced her way, an amused smirk tugging at her lips. "Try to act like you're not being dragged to your doom, Dani. It's just a bookshop."

Daniella raised an eyebrow. "I'll keep that in mind while you sit here in your perfect little bubble, baking cookies and judging me."

he tension in the room thickened as Maria's smile faltered. Their
other, ever the peacemaker, clapped her hands. "Girls, enough! It's
Christmas! Let's try to get along, please."

The journey to the bookshop was quiet, though not the comfortable
kind. Daniella stared out of the car window as her mother prattled on
about how much Mr. Peters needed help, while Maria remained
silent, clearly uninterested in the topic.

When they arrived, Daniella's first impression was…
underwhelming.

The shop was nestled between two taller buildings on a cobblestone
street in the heart of Dublin. Its peeling sign read Peters' Treasures,
though the faded letters looked more like a ghost of its former self.
Inside, the air smelled of dust and old paper. Books were crammed
haphazardly onto shelves that sagged under their weight. A rickety
ladder leaned against one wall, and the counter was buried under a
mountain of clutter—receipts, loose papers, and a mug that looked
like it hadn't been washed in years.

A frail man shuffled toward them from the back of the shop. Mr.
Peters.

"Ah, you must be Daniella," he said, his voice soft but warm. He
extended a trembling hand. "Thank you for coming. I was beginning
to think this place would be my tomb."

Daniella shook his hand, trying not to wince at the strength of his
grip despite his frailty. "Looks like you could use the help," she
said, surveying the chaos.

He laughed, a sound that felt oddly out of place in the dreary shop. "Yes, well, this old place has seen better days.

But it has a soul, you know? You can feel it, can't you?"

Daniella wasn't sure if she felt a soul or just an overwhelming urge to clean, but she nodded politely.

As her mother and Mr. Peters chatted, Daniella wandered deeper into the shop. The shelves seemed to close in around her, and the farther she walked, the darker the corners became. She swore she heard faint whispers, but every time she turned, no one was there.

In the back, she found a locked glass cabinet. Unlike the rest of the shop, it was spotless, its contents arranged with care. Inside were a dozen books, each bound in black leather and marked with strange, unreadable symbols.

"Don't touch those," Mr. Peters said, startling her. He was suddenly behind her, his gaze sharp. "Those books are… special. They're not for sale."

"Relax," Daniella said, raising her hands. "I wasn't planning on it."

He softened, but his tone was still firm. "Just be careful where you tread here. This shop has secrets, and not all of them are kind."

By the time they left, Daniella felt more drained than she'd expected. The shop's disarray wasn't just physical—it had a weight like it carried years of stories that weren't entirely finished.

As they drove back, her mother was all smiles, optimistic about the shop's potential. Maria, on the other hand, had that familiar smirk.

"Let me guess," she said. "You think the place is haunted."

Don't be ridiculous," Daniella snapped, though her unease lingered.

Maria laughed, and Daniella stared out the window, her thoughts swirling. Maybe Maria was right—maybe it was just an old shop. Or maybe, just maybe, Mr. Peter's warning wasn't just the ramblings of an eccentric old man.

Chapter Two: THE BOOKSHOP OF WHISPERS

"Every story begins with a whisper, but it's the echoes that shape its ending."

The next morning, Daniella returned to Peters' Treasures alone. Her mother had made an excuse about errands, and Maria simply waved her off with a half-hearted "good luck." Daniella wasn't sure if the words were genuine or another jab, but she didn't care.

The bell above the door tinkled as she entered, but the sound was almost swallowed by the oppressive quiet inside. The shop seemed darker than it had the previous day, the shadows longer, the air thicker. She hesitated for a moment before stepping in.

"Good, you're here." Mr. Peters emerged from behind the counter, holding a feather duster that looked older than she was. "The place is all yours today. Start wherever you like."

Daniella raised an eyebrow. "You're not helping?"

He chuckled, though there was no humor in it. "This old man's bones aren't what they used to be. I'll be in the back if you need me."

And just like that, he disappeared into the shadows, leaving her alone with the mess—and the whispers.

he hours crawled by as Daniella tackled the chaos one shelf at a
ne. Dust coated her hands, her clothes, her hair. The books seemed
 multiply as she worked, their spines marked with titles she didn't
cognize. Some were faded to the point of illegibility; others were
 languages she couldn't read.

ut it wasn't just the physical labor that unsettled her. It was the
eling of being watched.

very so often, she would catch movement out of the corner of her
re—a flicker of shadow, a shift in the light. And then there were
e whispers. Soft, almost imperceptible, but there.

he tried to ignore them at first, chalking it up to her imagination.
ut as the day went on, they grew louder, more distinct.

aniella… Daniella…

he spun around, her heart pounding. No one was there.

y late afternoon, she had made a small dent in the chaos. The front
 the shop looked marginally more presentable, and she even
anaged to organize a few of the shelves. But her curiosity kept
ılling her toward the locked cabinet in the back.

he books inside seemed to call to her, their strange symbols almost
owing in the dim light. She ran her fingers along the glass, feeling
strange hum of energy beneath her touch.

You're drawn to them, aren't you?"

aniella jumped, nearly knocking over a stack of books. Mr. Peters
ood behind her, his expression unreadable.

 wasn't—"

"It's alright," he said, cutting her off. "It's natural to be curious. Bu[t]
those books aren't like the others. They have a… presence."

"What kind of presence?" Daniella asked, crossing her arms.

He hesitated, then sighed. "They're part of this shop's history. Dark
history. That's all you need to know for now."

Daniella frowned, but she didn't push. Instead, she turned back to
the shelves and tried to focus on her work.

As the evening approached, a customer entered—a rare occurrence,
judging by Mr. Peters's surprised expression.

The man was tall, with sharp features and an air of confidence that
filled the room. His leather jacket and worn boots gave him a rugge[d]
charm, but there was something unsettling in his piercing blue eyes[.]

"James Calloway," he introduced himself, extending a hand to Mr.
Peters. "I'm an author. Heard this place might have some hidden
gems."

Daniella watched from a distance, her instincts tingling.

Mr. Peters forced a smile. "We have plenty of treasures, though not
all of them are for sale."

James's eyes flicked to the locked cabinet, lingering there for a
moment too long. "I've heard about your collection. Particularly th[e]
books in that case. Rare, aren't they?"

"They're not for sale," Mr. Peters said firmly.

James smiled, but it didn't reach his eyes. "Shame. I've always bee[n]
fascinated by the unusual."

After James left, Daniella couldn't shake the feeling that something
was off about him.

Who was that?" she asked Mr. Peters.

"Trouble," he said simply. "Stay away from him."

Daniella's curiosity flared. She wanted to know more—about James, about the cabinet, about the whispers that seemed to grow louder every time she looked at those books. But Mr. Peters had already retreated to the back room, leaving her with nothing but questions.

As she closed up the shop that evening, she paused by the cabinet one last time. The whispers were louder now, almost urgent.

Daniella… open the book…

She shivered, stepping away. Whatever secrets this shop held, she wasn't ready to face them. Not yet.

But deep down, she knew it was only a matter of time.

The next morning, Daniella arrived at the shop earlier than usual, clutching a cup of coffee and steeling herself for another long day. The whispers from the previous day still echoed faintly in her mind, but she brushed them off. Exhaustion, she told herself. Just exhaustion.

Mr. Peters was already there, humming an old tune as he dusted the counter. He looked brighter than usual, his frailty less pronounced.

"Morning, Daniella," he said with surprising cheer.

"Morning," she muttered, still half-asleep. "Anything specific you want me to work on today?"

He gestured toward a box of books near the counter.

"Catalog those. And if you have time, organize the back shelves. They've been neglected for years."

Daniella sighed, sipping her coffee. It wasn't glamorous work, but least it was straightforward.

As she sorted through the box, she noticed a pattern. Many of the books had handwritten notes in the margins, some in English, other in languages she didn't recognize. One book, bound in faded red leather, had a symbol etched into the cover—a jagged circle with an eye in the center.

She opened it carefully, the pages brittle with age. The handwriting inside was cramped and spidery, the ink faded to a rusty brown. It wasn't a language she understood, but the sight of it sent a chill down her spine.

"Interesting find, isn't it?"

Daniella jumped, nearly dropping the book. Mr. Peters was standing over her, his expression unreadable.

"What's this?" she asked, holding up the book.

He took it from her gently, running his fingers over the cover. "A journal, I believe. From the early days of this shop. Its original owner was… peculiar."

"Peculiar how?" Daniella asked, intrigued.

He hesitated, then gave her a thin smile. "Some stories are better le untold."

Before she could press further, he placed the book on a high shelf, out of reach.

The day passed uneventfully until the afternoon, when Maria arrived unexpectedly, her expression tight with annoyance.

"Mom sent me to check on you," she said, looking around the shop with thinly veiled disdain. "This place is… charming."

"Charming?" Daniella scoffed, gesturing to the chaos around them. "That's one word for it."

Maria ignored the jab, her eyes landing on the locked cabinet. "What's in there?"

"Books," Daniella replied. "Apparently, the special kind."

Maria frowned. "Special how?"

Before Daniella could answer, the bell above the door tinkled, and James Calloway strode in, his presence immediately filling the room.

"Ladies," he said with a charming smile. "Back again, I see."

Maria's eyes lit up at the sight of him, and Daniella resisted the urge to roll her eyes.

"James, right?" Maria said, stepping forward. "The author?"

"That's me," he said, shaking her hand. His gaze flicked to Daniella. "And you must be the one keeping this place alive."

"Something like that," Daniella muttered, crossing her arms.

James's smile widened. "I'd love to pick your brain sometime. Bookshops are fascinating, don't you think? So many stories hidden in plain sight."

Maria looked thoroughly charmed, but Daniella remained wary. There was something about James—something she couldn't quite put her finger on.

1

Later that evening, as the shop grew quiet, Daniella found herself drawn to the cabinet again. The whispers were louder now, almost urgent.

Open it… the answers are inside…

She tried to ignore them, but her hand moved of its own accord, reaching for the glass. To her surprise, it wasn't locked. The cabinet door swung open silently, revealing the black leather-bound books within.

Her fingers brushed the spine of one book, and a jolt of electricity shot through her arm. She yanked her hand back, her heart racing.

"What are you doing?"

Mr. Peters's voice cut through the silence like a knife. He was standing in the doorway, his face pale and furious.

"I—I thought it was locked," Daniella stammered.

"It should have been," he said, his voice trembling. "These books aren't toys, Daniella. They're dangerous."

"Dangerous how?" she asked, frustration bubbling up. "You keep saying things like that, but you never explain!"

He closed the cabinet, locking it this time. "Because some knowledge comes at too high a price. Let that be enough for you."

As she left the shop that night, Daniella couldn't shake the feeling that she had unlocked something—something that wouldn't be easily put back. The whispers followed her into the street, growing fainter with every step she took.

And in the shadows of the shop, something stirred.

Chapter Three: ECHOES IN THE DARK

"The shadows we fear often hold truths we cannot face."

Daniella woke in a cold sweat, her dream clinging to her like a second skin. In it, she was back in the bookshop, the whispers swirling around her, louder and clearer than ever. A shadowy figure stood behind the glass cabinet, its eyes glowing as it spoke her name.

She sat up in bed, her breath coming in shallow gasps. The room was dark except for the faint glow of Christmas lights from the window. But even those seemed dimmer, as though the darkness outside was pressing in.

Shaking off the remnants of the dream, she got dressed. She didn't want to go back to the shop—not after the way Mr. Peters had looked at her the previous night—but she had promised to help.

And part of her, the part she didn't want to admit existed, was drawn to the mystery.

The shop was eerily quiet when she arrived. The bell above the door tinkled, but it felt muted, as though the air itself was absorbing the sound.

"Mr. Peters?" she called, but there was no answer.

Frowning, she stepped inside. The shop felt different—darker, colder. The shelves seemed taller, the shadows deeper. She tried to shake off the unease, chalking it up to her imagination.

As she moved to the counter, she noticed a folded piece of paper resting on top.

Out for errands. Back soon. Don't touch the cabinet.

Daniella rolled her eyes, crumpling the note. "Yeah, because that worked so well last time."

Hours passed as she busied herself with reorganizing the shelves. But no matter how hard she tried to focus, her gaze kept drifting toward the cabinet. The black books inside seemed to hum with energy, their strange symbols almost pulsing in the dim light.

And the whispers—they were back, clearer than ever.

Daniella… we need you…

She slammed a book onto the counter, trying to block out the sound.

"Get a grip," she muttered to herself.

But the whispers didn't stop.

Open the cabinet… the truth is inside…

Before she could stop herself, she was walking toward the cabinet. The key was still in Mr. Peter's pocket, but the whispers urged her on, promising answers, promising power.

Her fingers brushed the glass, and the door swung open on its own. Inside, the books seemed to glow faintly, their symbols shifting and twisting like living things. She reached for the nearest one, her hand trembling.

he moment she touched it, a wave of cold rushed through her, and

e room seemed to tilt. She staggered back, clutching the book to

r chest as the whispers grew deafening.

nd then she heard it—a low, guttural laugh.

urning slowly, she saw a figure emerging from the shadows. It was

mes Calloway.

Well, well," he said, his voice smooth and mocking. "Looks like

u couldn't resist."

aniella stared at him, her heart racing. "What are you doing here?"

Same as you," he said, his eyes gleaming. "Looking for answers."

Answers to what?" she demanded.

To what this place really is," he replied, stepping closer. "To what

ose books really are."

e reached for the book in her hands, but she pulled back.

Don't," she said, her voice trembling. "Mr. Peters said—"

Mr. Peters doesn't want you to know the truth," James interrupted.

But you've felt it, haven't you? This shop is alive. Those books are

ive. And they've chosen you."

aniella shook her head, backing away. "You're insane."

Am I?" he asked, his smile widening. "Or am I the only one willing

 face the truth?"

efore she could respond, the shop seemed to shift around them.

he shelves groaned, the floorboards creaked, and the shadows

epened, swallowing the light.

The whispers turned into a roar, a cacophony of voices speaking in languages she couldn't understand. And then, out of the corner of her eye, she saw it—the shadowy figure from her dream.

It stood by the cabinet, its glowing eyes fixed on her.

"What… what is that?" she whispered.

James didn't answer. He was staring at the figure, his confidence replaced by fear.

The figure stepped forward, and Daniella felt a wave of cold wash over her. Its voice was deep and resonant, echoing in her mind.

You have taken what is not yours. You must face the consequences.

The book in her hands began to burn, its heat searing through her skin. She cried out, dropping it to the floor.

The figure extended a shadowy hand, and the book flew back into the cabinet, the door slamming shut behind it. The room fell silent, the oppressive weight lifting as quickly as it had come.

Daniella turned to James, her voice shaking. "What the hell just happened?"

He didn't answer. He was already backing away, his face pale.

"This isn't over," he said, his voice trembling. And then he was gone, leaving Daniella alone with the shadows.

When Mr. Peters returned, she didn't mention what had happened. But as she locked up the shop that night, she couldn't shake the feeling that she had crossed a line—that whateve secrets the shop held, they were no longer content to stay hidden.

…

he morning light struggled to penetrate the heavy clouds as
Daniella approached Peters' Treasures. The events of the previous
day clung to her like a bad dream, but the faint burn marks on her
hands were all too real. She had scrubbed them raw, but the
sensation lingered—a reminder of the strange energy she had felt
when she touched the book.

When she opened the door, the bell tinkled faintly, and Mr. Peters
glanced up from the counter, his expression weary.

"You're late," he said, though there was no real reproach in his tone.

"Long night," Daniella muttered, avoiding his gaze.

He studied her for a moment, then sighed. "Something happened,
didn't it?"

Daniella hesitated, the memory of the shadowy figure flashing in her
mind. "Nothing I can't handle," she said finally.

Mr. Peters frowned but didn't press further. Instead, he slid a cup of
tea across the counter. "You'll need your strength. We've got a busy
day ahead."

The shop filled with an unusual bustle that morning. Customers
came and went, most of them drawn to the newly organized shelves.
Daniella found herself surprisingly absorbed in the work, her unease
pushed to the back of he mind.

But the whispers didn't leave her. They hovered at the edge of her
hearing, soft and insistent.

By midday, she couldn't ignore them anymore. She ducked into the
back room, hoping for a moment of quiet.

The whispers followed her.

He knows… you must ask him…

She spun around, half-expecting to see the shadowy figure from before. But the room was empty, save for the stacks of books and the faint smell of dust.

Taking a deep breath, she stepped back into the front of the shop. Mr. Peters was helping an older woman find a rare edition of a poetry book, his demeanor calm and patient.

When the customer left, Daniella approached him. "We need to talk."

He looked up, his expression guarded. "About what?"

"The cabinet," she said, lowering her voice. "And the books inside it. What's really going on here?"

Mr. Peters sighed, running a hand through his thinning hair. "I was hoping it wouldn't come to this."

He led her into the back room and closed the door behind them. For a moment, he simply stood there, as though gathering his thoughts.

"This shop," he began, "is older than it looks. And it's not just a place for selling books. It's a repository—a vault, if you will—for things that shouldn't be out in the world."

Daniella frowned. "What kind of things?"

He gestured toward the locked cabinet. "Books that were never meant to be written. Stories that hold power—real power. They're dangerous, Daniella. And they have a way of calling out to people."

She thought of the whispers, the way they had drawn her to the cabinet. "Calling out… like voices?"

Mr. Peters nodded grimly. "You've heard them, haven't you?"

28

he nodded, the weight of the admission settling in her chest. "Why me? Why not you or someone else?"

"Because the shop chooses," he said simply. "It has its own will, its own purpose. And for some reason, it's chosen you."

Daniella didn't know how to respond to that. She sank into a nearby chair, her mind racing.

"James Calloway," she said suddenly. "He's involved in this, isn't he?"

Mr. Peters's expression darkened. "James is… persistent. He's been after the books for years. Thinks he can use them to fuel his writing. But he doesn't understand the cost."

"What cost?" Daniella asked.

Mr. Peters hesitated. "The books demand something in return. They give knowledge, yes, but they take something, too. Your sanity, your soul, your life—it varies. But the price is always steep."

The room seemed to grow colder, the shadows pressing in around them.

"So what am I supposed to do?" Daniella asked, her voice barely above a whisper.

Mr. Peters placed a hand on her shoulder. "Stay away from the cabinet. Stay away from James. And, above all, trust your instincts. They'll be your best defense."

That evening, Daniella closed up the shop alone. The whispers were louder now, more insistent.

Don't trust him… he's hiding something…

As she locked the door, she noticed a piece of paper tucked into the frame. It was a note, scrawled in a messy hand.

"Meet me tonight. There's more you need to know. —James."

Her heart pounded as she crumpled the note in her hand. The streetlights cast long shadows across the cobblestones, and the cold night air seemed to wrap around her like a shroud.

She glanced back at the shop, its windows dark and uninviting. The whispers were right about one thing: someone was hiding something.

And she was determined to find out what.

Daniella stood in the cold night air, the crumpled note from James still clenched in her hand. The streets of Dublin were quiet, the usual cheer of holiday lights doing little to pierce the oppressive feeling that had settled over her.

"Meet me tonight," the note had said. But could she trust him?

The memory of his fear in the shop earlier lingered in her mind. He knew something—something Mr. Peters wasn't telling her. If there were answers to be found, she wasn't about to turn away now.

The meeting point was an old stone bridge on the edge of the city. Daniella arrived early, her breath visible in the frosty air. The river below was calm, its surface reflecting the dim glow of streetlights.

…

James emerged from the shadows moments later, his usual smug confidence replaced by a tense urgency.

"You came," he said, his voice low.

et's skip the pleasantries," Daniella replied, crossing her arms.
What do you want?"

mes hesitated, glancing around as though checking for
vesdroppers. "There's more to this shop than Peters will ever
lmit. He's hiding things—dangerous things."

he frowned. "You mean the books? He already told me they're
ngerous."

mes shook his head. "It's not just the books. The shop itself… it's
ive. It's connected to something ancient, something that goes
yond anything you can imagine."

aniella stared at him, her skepticism warring with the memory of
e shadowy figure and the whispers. "And you know this
cause…?"

've been researching it for years," he said, stepping closer. "The
op, the books, the symbols—they're all part of a larger puzzle. A
tual that's been forgotten by most but still lingers in places like
is."

Ritual?" she repeated, her pulse quickening.

mes nodded. "The books aren't just dangerous; they're a key.
ogether, they can open a door—a door to a power beyond
omprehension. But someone has to complete the ritual to make it
ppen."

aniella's stomach churned. "And you think Mr. Peters is planning
 do that?"

"I don't know," James admitted. "But I know he's hiding something. The books are locked away for a reason, and he's desperate to keep them out of reach."

…

A gust of wind swept over the bridge, making Daniella shiver. "If this ritual is so dangerous, why are you so interested in it?"

James hesitated, his expression conflicted. "Because power like that can't just be ignored. If someone else gets to it first…"

He trailed off, and Daniella felt a chill that had nothing to do with the weather.

"So what do you want from me?" she asked finally.

"I need your help," James said. "You've already touched one of the books. That means the shop has chosen you. It's connected to you now."

She shook her head, stepping back. "No. I'm not getting involved in whatever this is."

"You already are," James said quietly. "Whether you like it or not."

Daniella turned away, her mind racing. She wanted to dismiss him as a lunatic, but too much had happened in the past few days to ignore.

"Be careful, Daniella," James called after her. "Peters isn't who you think he is."

She didn't look back.

When she returned to the shop the next morning, Mr. Peters was waiting for her. His expression was unreadable, but there was a tension in his posture that hadn't been there before.

"You met with him," he said, his tone flat.

Daniella froze. "How did you—"

"This shop hears everything," he interrupted. "It sees everything. And it knows when its secrets are at risk."

She swallowed hard, the weight of his words sinking in. "James said you're hiding something. That you're planning to use the books for ritual."

Mr. Peter's expression darkened. "James doesn't understand what he's playing with. The books aren't a key—they're a prison. And if they're opened, they'll unleash something no one can control."

"Then why keep them here?" Daniella demanded.

"Because this is the only place that can contain them," he replied. "But the containment is fragile. If you or James keep meddling, it won't hold."

The tension between them was palpable, and for the first time, Daniella felt truly afraid. The shop wasn't just a quaint, dusty relic of the past—it was a battleground.

And she was caught in the middle.

Daniella's mind raced as she left the shop. She had barely registered Mr. Peter's warning before she stepped out into the biting cold of the Dublin morning. The air felt sharper, heavier somehow, as though the world itself were holding its breath.

3

The meeting with James had unsettled her more than she cared to admit. There were pieces of the puzzle she hadn't understood yet, but something in her gut told her that she was closer to a truth she might not be ready to face.

The shop isn't what it seems, James had said.

Mr. Peters is hiding something.

And then there were the whispers. They'd started again—softer at first, then louder as she walked away. Their voices seemed to come from everywhere and nowhere all at once.

The door is open. You can feel it. It's waiting for you.

She shook her head, trying to block them out. But the closer she got to the shop, the more they seemed to follow her.

When she arrived at Peters' Treasures, the door was slightly ajar, the bell silent as she pushed it open. The shop was quieter than usual, the shelves almost unnervingly still.

A soft rustling from the back room caught her attention.

"Mr. Peters?" she called.

There was no response.

Tentatively, she walked toward the back, each step echoing in the silence. The room beyond the counter was dimly lit, the only light coming from the flickering overhead bulb.

As she stepped closer to the cabinet, she froze.

The lock was broken. The door to the cabinet was slightly ajar.

No.

The whispers grew louder, urging her forward.

It's time. Open it.

Without thinking, Daniella reached for the door, her fingers brushing against the cold wood. The moment her hand made contact, the room seemed to shift—darker, colder.

Suddenly, the whispers stopped. The silence was deafening. She hesitated, her heart pounding. But before she could step away, the door to the back room creaked open, and Mr. Peters stepped inside. His face was pale, his eyes wide with something she couldn't quite read.

"No," he said, his voice tight with panic. "Daniella, don't open it. You don't know what you're doing."

But it was too late.

The cabinet door swung open with a low groan, revealing the books inside—row upon row of ancient, leather-bound volumes. The symbols on their spines seemed to shift and change, twisting in ways that made her stomach churn.

"You've awakened us.

The voice was deep, powerful, and chilling. It wasn't coming from the books—it was coming from within them.

Daniella stumbled back, her breath catching in her throat. "What is that?"

Mr. Peters rushed forward, slamming the cabinet door shut with a force that made the shelves tremble. "You have no idea what you've just unleashed," he muttered, his voice filled with regret.

The room seemed to spin, and Daniella grabbed onto the counter for support. The whispers were gone, replaced by an ominous, almost palpable silence.

"Why didn't you tell me?" she demanded, her voice shaking. "Why
didn't you warn me about what's in there?"

Mr. Peters' face was grim as he slowly sank into a chair. "I thought
could contain it. I thought if I kept the books locked away, I could
keep them from affecting anyone else. But now…" He shook his
head. "It's too late. You've opened the door, and now they're
awake."

"Who?" she asked, her voice barely a whisper.

"The ones who were trapped inside," he said, his eyes darkening.
"The ones who wrote the books. The ones whose power was sealed
away long ago. You've set them free, and they won't stop until
they've claimed what's theirs."

A chill settled over Daniella's bones as the weight of his words hit
her. She had always known there was something off about the shop,
but this… this was something beyond anything she could have
imagined.

She glanced at the cabinet again, but it seemed so innocuous now, s
ordinary, as if nothing had changed.

But she knew better.

The shop, the books, the whispers—they were all connected. And
now, there was no turning back.

"I have to go," she said abruptly, the need to escape surging through
her.

Mr. Peters didn't try to stop her. He merely watched as she grabbed
her coat and rushed toward the door.

The cold air hit her like a slap when she stepped outside, but even the biting wind couldn't shake the feeling that something was watching her.

The moment she turned the corner onto the cobblestone street, she heard it again—the whisper.

You can't run from what you've awakened.

Daniella froze, her heart pounding. She spun around, but the street was empty, the shadows deepening as the sun dipped below the horizon.

For the first time since this all began, Daniella felt truly terrified.

She had uncovered something ancient, something evil—and there was no telling how far the reach of the books would extend.

And worse still, she wasn't the only one looking for answers.

That night, as Daniella lay in bed, trying to shake the feeling that something was lurking just beyond her vision, her phone buzzed.

It was a message from James.

Meet me at the bridge. Now.

She stared at the screen for a long moment before typing a response.

Why? What do you know?

His reply came almost immediately.

You don't know what you've done. But I do. And we need to stop it.

Daniella's blood ran cold.

If James knew what she had just awakened, then it was worse than she thought.

She didn't want to go. But she knew she had no choice.

Chapter Four: THE PRICE OF KNOWLEDGE

"Sometimes, to understand the truth, you must first confront the darkness within yourself."

Daniella stood in front of the mirror, her reflection barely visible in the dim light. The world outside seemed to have faded, as though her very existence was suspended between two realities—the mundane world she had once known, and the one she had just stepped into.

The message from James weighed heavily on her mind. We need to stop it. What did he mean by that? What could they possibly do to undo what had been set in motion?

She pulled on her coat, her fingers trembling as she buttoned it up. The whispers were louder now, gnawing at the edges of her thoughts, urging her forward.

It's not over yet. You haven't seen the price.

She closed her eyes, taking a deep breath, trying to steady herself. The night outside was cold and still, the moon casting long shadows across the streets of Dublin.

James had insisted on meeting at the bridge again. She didn't know if it was fear or curiosity that drove her, but something in her gut old her this encounter would reveal more than she was ready to face.

The bridge loomed ahead, its stone arches looming like silent sentinels in the dark. As Daniella approached, she saw James standing at the far end, his posture rigid, his gaze fixed on the water below.

"You came," he said without turning around, his voice low and tense.

"I didn't have a choice," Daniella replied, her voice tight.

James turned to face her, his eyes shadowed with something she couldn't quite place—fear, perhaps, or guilt. "You have no idea what you've done."

Daniella's heart skipped a beat. "What do you mean? What's going on? What are we dealing with here?"

James took a step closer, his expression hardening. "The books weren't just written for knowledge. They were created to trap something—something ancient. And the moment you opened that cabinet, you released it. You've given it power."

Daniella recoiled, the weight of his words sinking in. "What are you talking about? What did I release?"

The spirits," James said, his voice barely above a whisper. "The ones who wrote the books. They aren't just authors—they were… sorcerers, mystics. And they didn't just write for knowledge. They wrote to bind themselves to the books, to live on through them. They're trapped in the pages, Daniella.

They've been waiting for someone to open that door, to release them. And now you've done it."

Daniella felt the ground beneath her shift. "No, no, this can't be happening." She took a step back, her eyes wide with disbelief. "You're telling me that the books are alive? That they're haunting the shop?"

James nodded, his jaw clenched. "They're not ghosts, not exactly. But they hold power. Dark, ancient power. And that power is now awake. It wants to be freed. But if that happens… everything changes."

"How do you know all this?" Daniella asked, her voice trembling.

"I've been following the trail for years," James admitted, his eyes darkening. "Peters has been keeping the books hidden for decades. He's the keeper, the one who holds the key to keeping them contained. But he's weak. He's aging, and I think… I think he's losing control."

Daniella shook her head, trying to process what James had just revealed. "So, what now? What do we do?"

James's expression hardened, and for a moment, Daniella saw a flicker of something desperate in his eyes. "We need to stop the ritual before it's completed. But we can't do it alone. The books have already started to influence people. There's a force building, and if we don't stop it now, we'll all be part of it."

Daniella clenched her fists, frustration boiling inside her. "How do we stop it? What do we do?"

mes's voice dropped to a whisper. "There's only one way. We
eed to burn the books. Destroy them. But that means facing the
ing inside them. The entity that's been waiting all this time."

aniella felt the weight of his words crush her chest. "Burn them?
ow are we supposed to even get close? If they're as powerful as
ou say…"

We'll have to find a way," James said, determination in his eyes.
The longer we wait, the stronger it gets. We don't have much
me."

st as Daniella was about to speak again, a shadow shifted across
e bridge. She turned, her heart skipping a beat as she saw Mr.
eters standing at the far end, watching them. His face was pale, his
ands trembling at his sides.

You shouldn't be here," Daniella said, stepping back. "What are
ou doing?"

r. Peters didn't respond immediately. Instead, his gaze flickered
ward James before turning back to Daniella. "I had hoped to keep
ou away from this, but now…" He paused, his eyes clouded with a
ix of fear and regret. "You've set things in motion, Daniella. And
ow you must finish it."

Finish what?" Daniella demanded, her voice rising. "Finish what,
r. Peters?"

e took a deep breath, his hands clenched at his sides. "The ritual
n't just about the books. It's about you. It was always about you.
ou're the key."

aniella's breath caught in her throat. "What do you mean?"

"You have the power to stop it," Mr. Peters said softly, his voice breaking. "But it's not a power you can control. Not easily."

James stepped forward, his face pale with realization. "You knew, didn't you? You knew all along that Daniella was the one who could destroy it, but you kept her in the dark."

Mr. Peters's eyes met Daniella's, and for the first time, she saw the true weight of the years he had carried. "I didn't want you to have to make this choice. But now you must. Because the price of knowledge is steep—and the cost is your soul."

Daniella felt her knees buckle, the weight of his words threatening to crush her. "What price? What are you saying?!"

"The price is you," Mr. Peters whispered. "Only you can close the door, but you'll never be the same. You will either be consumed by the darkness, or you will give everything to stop it."

Daniella's world tilted. She felt a wave of nausea wash over her, the reality of what she was being asked to do closing in.

She could feel the power in the books—feel it trying to reach her. It was too late to walk away now. The whispers were louder than ever. The entity was here, and she was its last hope.

Daniella stood at the center of the bridge, the cold night air biting at her skin, but it was nothing compared to the chill she felt in her bones. The weight of Mr. Peter's words hung heavily in the air. The price of knowledge is steep—and the cost is your soul.

Her mind spun as the sounds of the world around her faded into the background, the voices in her head growing louder.

It's you. You're the key.

he could feel the presence of something ancient, something powerful, watching her, waiting for her to make the choice. The choice she had no idea she was meant to make until now.

James stood to the side, his expression grim. "You don't have to do this, Daniella. There's always another way." His voice was filled with a mixture of hope and desperation, but Daniella could see the flicker of fear in his eyes.

"I'm not sure I even understand what's happening anymore," she whispered, shaking her head as she paced. "I opened a door I shouldn't have, and now there's no going back. But what if there's no way to stop this?"

Mr. Peters stepped closer, his eyes dark with the burden of years of secrets. "There is no way to stop it without you, Daniella. The ritual can only be undone if you make the sacrifice. You are the one the books have chosen."

"Chosen?" Daniella scoffed bitterly. "Chosen for what? To be a vessel for whatever dark force is lurking in those pages? To end up like the authors who bound themselves to those books, forever enslaved?"

Mr. Peters didn't answer. He didn't have to. The truth hung in the air like an unspoken curse.

Daniella's heart raced, her breath quickening as the weight of the situation bore down on her. She glanced back at the shop, the place that had drawn her in with its strange allure, its creaking shelves and endless rows of old books. The shop had become more than just a place. It was a prison—one that had ensnared her in a way she couldn't explain.

"What do you mean, I'm the key?" Daniella asked, her voice barely a whisper, but the words echoed in the silent night.

James shook his head, his hand tightening into a fist at his side. "The shop is alive because of you. The books… they're connected to you in a way that no one understands. It's not just about power; it's about control. The books were created to enslave people like us, Daniella. But you're different. They know you."

"You've heard the voices too," Daniella said slowly, finally understanding. "You've felt it, haven't you? They're calling to us." James didn't answer, but the look in his eyes told her everything she needed to know.

"The power in the books is too great," Mr. Peters interjected, his voice hoarse. "It cannot be allowed to spread. The ritual isn't just about opening a door—it's about binding the power back into the books. But it can't be done without you. You must choose."

Daniella felt the weight of the decision crushing her chest. To close the door, to stop the ritual, she would have to destroy everything— the shop, the books, the source of the power that had lured her in from the start. But that destruction would come with a cost. She could feel it in the pit of her stomach, a growing darkness that was waiting to consume her.

It was a choice between giving herself over to the darkness and risking the very soul of everyone she loved, or sacrificing herself to top it from spreading. Either way, she was bound to lose omething.

'I can't…" Daniella whispered, her eyes darting between the two nen, desperate for some other option. "I can't be the one to end it ill."

'You have no choice," Mr. Peters said quietly. "If you don't, the itual will be completed. The power will rise, and the world will be wallowed in its wake. It will never stop until everything is consumed."

Daniella's heart beat wildly in her chest. "What if I don't have the trength to finish it? What if I can't stop the darkness once it starts?"

'You must," James said, his voice steady but filled with urgency. 'The books will try to take you, but you're stronger than they think. The power in you—it's your choice whether you control it or it controls you. But you have to decide now."

The wind howled around them, but all Daniella could hear was her own breathing and the pounding of her heart. She felt the weight of a thousand eyes on her, the books watching, waiting, as if they knew what she was about to do.

She turned to face James, her eyes searching his face. "And you? What will you do if I make the sacrifice? What happens to you?"

James took a deep breath. "I'll be here, Daniella. I'll make sure the books don't claim anyone else. But this is something you have to do alone."

The truth of his words hit her with the force of a sledgehammer. This wasn't about anyone else. This was her battle, her choice.

45

And yet…

And yet…

The air around her seemed to pulse with an otherworldly energy, and Daniella knew, deep down, that she was the only one who could do this. The whispers were becoming frantic, urging her to step forward, to embrace the darkness and the power it promised. But the weight of the choice was suffocating.

"I'm not strong enough," she whispered, her eyes clouded with doubt.

"You are," Mr. Peters said softly, his voice filled with something close to sorrow. "You're stronger than you know. The books have taken enough from us. It's time to take back control."

Daniella took a deep breath, and for the first time since all of this began, she felt the stirrings of courage. She wasn't going to let the darkness win. She wasn't going to let it consume her.

She looked at the two men—at James, whose fate was now tied to hers, and at Mr. Peters, who had carried this burden for too long—and made her choice.

With a final, shuddering breath, she turned toward the shop. She had made the decision. Now she had to face what came next.

Daniella stepped into the shop, the air thick with a sense of foreboding. The books seemed to watch her, their leather covers worn with age, their pages filled with secrets she had yet to understand. The whispers were louder now, echoing in her mind like a thousand voices calling her name, urging her to take the next step.

ames and Mr. Peters followed her into the shop, but they kept their distance. Daniella felt like the weight of the world rested on her shoulders, every step she took drawing her closer to the final choice. The ritual was near completion. She could feel it in the air, the electricity that hummed just beneath the surface of her skin.

The candlelight flickered ominously as she walked through the aisles, her eyes scanning the shelves for the books that had started it all. The ones that were both the source and the key to stopping the ritual. She could feel the presence of the entity—an ancient power, more vast and terrifying than anything she had ever imagined.

Do you have the book?" Daniella asked, her voice shaky but resolute.

James hesitated before pulling a large, dusty tome from his bag.

This is the one. The Book of Shadows. It contains the final instructions for the ritual."

Daniella took the book from him, her hands trembling as she opened the heavy cover. The pages were filled with strange symbols and drawings, words written in languages she couldn't recognize. She could almost hear the voices within, urging her to turn the pages faster, to read the incantations that would seal her fate.

Daniella…" Mr. Peters's voice was strained, his hands clasped tightly in front of him. "You have to be sure. Once you begin, there's no turning back. The entity will try to stop you. It will use everything in its power to keep you from completing the ritual."

She nodded, her resolve hardening. She had come too far to back down now. She could feel the power growing, the darkness rising around her. The entity was close, so close that it almost seemed to breathe down her neck.

"I'm ready," Daniella said, her voice barely a whisper, but it rang with determination.

With a deep breath, she began to chant the words written on the page, the strange syllables flowing from her lips as if they were a part of her. The air in the shop grew heavy, the walls creaking as the entity stirred, its presence growing stronger with every word Daniella spoke.

Suddenly, a cold wind swept through the shop, and the shadows in the corners seemed to grow deeper, darker. The books began to rattle on their shelves, as though they were alive, shaking with the power of the entity trapped within them. Daniella could feel the power surge within her, her skin tingling as if she were plugged into an unseen source.

"No!" a voice roared from the darkness. "You cannot stop me!" Daniella's heart raced as she turned toward the source of the voice, but there was no one there. The entity had no physical form—it was in the books, in the very air around her, and it was growing stronger by the second.

"Keep going, Daniella!" James shouted, his voice filled with urgency. "Don't stop! You have to finish it!"

She nodded, forcing herself to focus. The ritual was almost complete, but she could feel the power of the books pushing back against her, fighting to prevent the ritual from succeeding. She could sense the entity's anger, its desperation to remain free.

he shop seemed to close in around her, the walls narrowing, the ceiling lowering. The books were no longer just words—they were alive, pulsing with energy, as though they were hungry for something. They were feeding on the power she was channeling, trying to take it from her.

With a final burst of strength, Daniella finished the chant, the last words pouring from her mouth like a torrent. The books seemed to scream as the power surged through her, the entity's presence shuddering and weakening. She could feel it—the darkness receding, retreating back into the pages from which it had come.

The shop fell silent, the oppressive atmosphere lifting as if a weight had been removed. The books, now still and silent, no longer thrummed with the dark energy they had once contained. The ritual was over. The darkness had been sealed.

But Daniella didn't feel victorious. Her body trembled with exhaustion, her head spinning from the overwhelming energy she had just channeled. She had won—but at what cost?

James rushed to her side, his eyes wide with relief. "You did it. It's over."

Mr. Peters stepped forward, his face grim. "The ritual is complete, but you've paid the price."

Daniella looked at him, her chest heavy with the weight of his words. "What do you mean? What price?"

The books… the power they contained…" Mr. Peter's voice faltered. "You've sealed it away, but the darkness has taken something from you. Something you'll never get back."

Daniella looked down at her hands, feeling the lingering power within them. It was as though a part of her had been ripped away. She felt hollow, empty, and yet the world around her seemed to hav shifted into focus. The shop was still there, the books still stood on their shelves, but everything had changed.

"Are you okay?" James asked, his concern evident.

Daniella looked up at him, her voice quiet but firm. "I don't know. I don't feel the same."

Mr. Peters nodded, his eyes filled with sorrow. "None of us do. The books take more than you realize. They never give up their power without exacting a toll."

The shop seemed quieter now, its oppressive atmosphere replaced with a sense of finality. The entity was gone, but the price had been paid. Daniella felt it in her very bones, a lingering ache that would never go away.

As they stood there in the silence, Daniella realized one thing: the darkness might have been sealed, but it had left its mark. And so had she.

Chapter Five: BENEATH THE SURFACE

"The surface may be calm, but beneath it, the storm is waiting. Only by diving deep can we find the truth."

The cold, damp air of the bookshop seemed to press against Daniella's skin like a heavy blanket, suffocating in its stillness. The shop was no longer filled with the throbbing pulse of the entity—it was silent, almost too silent. The oppressive atmosphere had lifted, but in its place was something just as unsettling: a quiet that hummed with the echo of what had just transpired.

Daniella stood in the center of the room, her breath slow and steady, her eyes fixed on the shelves that seemed to mock her with their calm. The books no longer rattled with the force of the dark energy that had once kept them alive.

But she couldn't shake the feeling that something was off, something hidden just beneath the surface of this newfound calm.

James stood next to her, his hand hesitating as if unsure whether to reach out. "You did it. The entity is gone. It's over."

His voice was filled with relief, but there was a certain distance in his eyes. Daniella could see the tension in his posture, the tightness of his jaw. He wanted to believe it was over. He wanted to believe she had saved them all. But she could tell he was just as unsure as she was.

"I don't feel like I've won," Daniella whispered, the words escaping her before she could stop them. "Something doesn't feel right."

James's expression faltered. "What do you mean?"

"I'm not the same," she replied, her voice filled with an eerie certainty. "The darkness—it took something from me. Not just my energy, but… something deeper."

Mr. Peters had retreated to the far corner of the shop, his back turned to them as he sifted through a stack of old books. His face was drawn and pale, a far cry from the man who had once seemed so sure of himself. Daniella knew he had been part of this—the ritual, the books, everything. And now, it seemed that the toll was not just hers to pay.

"It's not just you," he said softly, his voice tinged with regret. "The books don't let you walk away unscathed. I've known that for years. But I thought… I thought we could contain it."

"Contain it?" Daniella's voice was sharp now, the remnants of frustration and disbelief mixing with a dark realization. "We didn't contain anything. We only stopped it temporarily."

Mr. Peters didn't look up, his voice a low murmur. "Perhaps. But you've done more than anyone else. The books are sealed, at least for now."

"Sealed?" Daniella echoed. She took a step closer to him, her pulse quickening. "What happens when they're unsealed? When they're opened again? This won't be over, will it?"

No," Mr. Peters admitted, finally meeting her gaze. "It won't be over. But it will be different. The darkness can't rise again without the key. And now, that key is yours."

Daniella's stomach turned as she processed his words. The key. She was the key.

Don't you see?" Mr. Peters said, his eyes darkening with the weight of years of secrets. "The books have always needed someone—someone who could channel their power, control it. That was never supposed to be you. But you were drawn to the books. The entity chose you. And now, it has left its mark."

You're saying I'm cursed?" Daniella's voice cracked with a bitter laugh. "Is that what this is?"

You're not cursed, but you're not free either," Mr. Peters replied, his voice heavy with sorrow. "The books have a way of marking their chosen ones. Their influence lingers, even when the darkness is gone. You may not see it now, but in time, you'll feel the change."

The words settled heavily in the air, and Daniella could almost feel the weight of them crushing her chest. She didn't want to believe it. She didn't want to think that she had been marked by something so ancient, so powerful, that it would never truly leave her. But deep down, she knew.

She had always known. She had always been drawn to the books— compelled, even. And now, no matter how much she wished it, the truth was undeniable. She would never be the same.

I want to go home," Daniella said suddenly, her voice raw with exhaustion. "I just want to go home and forget all of this."

But she knew, as soon as the words left her mouth, that she couldn't The books had changed her. The ritual had changed her. There was no going back.

James seemed to sense her need for solitude, and for the first time in days, he didn't try to comfort her. He simply nodded, his expression softening with understanding. He turned to leave, but Daniella caught his arm.

"James," she said, her voice quiet. "The books… they won't stop, will they? They'll find a way back. And when they do, it'll be worse."

He hesitated, then nodded grimly. "I know. I know. But we'll figure it out. We'll do whatever it takes."

Daniella watched as James left the shop, the door swinging shut behind him with a hollow thud. The silence that followed was deafening. The shop, once alive with dark energy, now felt like a tomb. She could almost feel the books watching her, waiting for her next move.

As she stood there, alone in the dim light of the shop, she realized one harsh truth: the battle wasn't over. It had only just begun. And now, she was not only a part of the story—she was its key.

Daniella couldn't sleep. Every time she closed her eyes, the whispers from the books returned, like a relentless tide crashing against her mind. The air in the shop felt thick, as though it had absorbed the very essence of the ritual, and now, it pulsed with a quiet, menacing energy.

he had thought that sealing the entity away would be the end of it. But the truth, bitter and unavoidable, gnawed at her: the power of the books was still there, still alive in some form. She had sealed the entity, yes—but it had left its mark on her, a scar that refused to fade.

The dark energy within her stirred again as she paced the shop, the shelves towering above her like silent witnesses to her internal battle. Each book seemed to whisper to her, their voices rising and falling in an eerie rhythm that felt like a heartbeat. It's not over, they seemed to chant. You belong to us now.

James's words from earlier echoed in her mind. "The books can't be opened again without the key." Daniella's chest tightened as she realized the full weight of that statement. She was the key. And that meant she wasn't just the one who had sealed the darkness away; she was the one who had been chosen to keep it from ever breaking free again.

But the books weren't done with her yet.

With a sudden, overwhelming urge, Daniella turned toward the back of the shop, toward the dusty, forgotten section of the store where the oldest, most dangerous books were kept. She had avoided them since the ritual—too afraid of what might lie hidden in their pages. But something deep inside her called to them now. A dark curiosity tugged at her, beckoning her closer.

Her fingers brushed against the worn spines, and she felt a chill run through her body. The books seemed to hum beneath her touch, their energy like a magnet, pulling her in. She couldn't resist.

As her hands ran over the pages of the oldest tome, something shifted in the air. A soft gasp escaped her lips as the cover creaked open by itself. The room around her seemed to distort, the walls bending and twisting as though they were alive, reacting to her every move.

The pages of the book fluttered as if a wind were blowing through them, yet the air was still. Each page was filled with symbols she couldn't read, but their power was undeniable. The words seemed to burn into her consciousness, the very ink written in them shifting, reshaping as they revealed things she wasn't meant to see.

A vision flashed before her eyes.

It was a memory—or was it a vision of something that had never happened? A place that looked strangely familiar, yet far older than anything she had ever known. The streets were narrow, winding, and cobbled, the buildings towering above her with an eerie, looming presence. A sense of dread filled the air, a quiet, whispering darkness hanging over everything.

She saw a figure, cloaked in shadows, standing at the entrance of an ancient library. And then, the figure turned to her, its face obscured, but its eyes glowing with a familiar, terrifying light. It was as though the darkness itself had a face.

Daniella stumbled back, her breath catching in her throat. The vision faded as quickly as it had come, but the feeling lingered. It was like something ancient had been awakened, something tied to the very essence of the books.

The entity wasn't gone. It was still out there, and it had left a piece of itself inside her.

Her head throbbed with the weight of what she had seen. The books, she realized, were not just vessels for dark power. They were linked to something far older, something rooted in the very foundation of the world. And it was using her to get what it wanted.

She could feel the connection now. The books were calling to her again, not with the same commanding force they had before, but with an eerie, almost seductive pull.

She couldn't stop herself from reaching for another book, one that seemed to call to her more strongly than the rest. As her fingers touched its cover, a strange warmth spread through her body, and she could hear the voice again.

You're one of us. You always have been.

The room around her darkened once again, and for a moment, Daniella felt her connection to the books deepen. The air felt heavy with their presence, the very walls of the shop seeming to pulse with the energy of the entity she had once sealed away.

But this time, it was different.

The energy didn't feel like an external force anymore. It felt like it was a part of her. She could almost see the threads of darkness that had woven their way into her soul, binding her to the books, to the entity.

She had thought she had sealed it. But the truth was that she had only delayed it. The darkness had never truly left. And now, she was a part of it.

She slammed the book shut, her heart pounding in her chest. She had to resist. She had to break free. But the pull was too strong.

"Daniella?" James's voice called from the doorway.

She turned to find him standing there, his face drawn with concern. "You okay?"

For a moment, Daniella just stared at him, the words caught in her throat. She wanted to tell him what she had seen, what she had felt, but the words wouldn't come. It was too much. Too much to bear.

"I—" she began, but then the words faltered. How could she explain what had just happened? How could she explain that the darkness inside her was only growing stronger?

She shook her head, her mind a whirlwind of confusion and fear. "I don't know what's happening, James. I thought I could stop it. I thought I could be rid of it."

James stepped forward, his hand resting gently on her shoulder. "Daniella, we'll figure this out. Together. You're not alone in this."

She looked up at him, her eyes filled with uncertainty. "What if I can't control it, James? What if it's already too late?"

He met her gaze, his eyes filled with determination. "We'll find a way. You're stronger than you think."

But as Daniella looked into his eyes, she couldn't shake the feeling that even he didn't truly understand what she was up against. The books, the entity—it wasn't something that could be defeated with strength or willpower alone. It was something much darker. And the truth was, Daniella wasn't sure if she could resist it much longer.

Daniella couldn't shake the nagging sensation that something had shifted inside her. The vision, the whispers, the eerie tug toward the books—they were no longer just figments of a nightmare. They were part of her reality now.

She tried to ignore it. She tried to focus on the small victories—the quiet hours of the shop, the peace of the customers who still wandered in, none the wiser to the malevolent forces that had once thrived in the shelves. But the whispers, always just below the surface, kept tugging at her. They were louder now, and the pull toward the books was no longer a fleeting temptation—it was an urgent, almost desperate need.

James's presence in the shop had become a comfort in the days following the ritual, but even his company couldn't erase the tension that had settled over Daniella like a dark fog. Each day, she woke up with the distinct sense that something was wrong, that she was no longer in control of her life. The books, once inert, now felt like a living, breathing thing in the back of her mind, whispering to her when the world was quiet.

As the days passed, her obsession deepened. She couldn't help but return to the books again and again, drawn by a force she could no longer deny. One night, she found herself standing before the shelf of forbidden tomes, her fingers twitching as they hovered over a particularly old and faded book. She could feel the energy radiating from it, the promise of knowledge and power.

One more. Just one more book, and I'll be done with it all. I'll understand everything.

Without thinking, Daniella pulled the book from the shelf, her heart pounding in her chest. As she opened it, the familiar hum of dark power filled the room, wrapping around her like a suffocating embrace. The words seemed to leap from the page, dancing before her eyes, their meanings twisting and reshaping like they were alive. They were calling to her, offering her something more, something she didn't yet understand.

It was then that she felt it—a cold, icy chill sweeping through the room, as if the very air itself had turned against her. The darkness, the entity, had returned. But this time, it wasn't just a force contained within the books. It was inside her. It was using her to manifest once again.

"Daniella!" James's voice cut through the fog of darkness surrounding her. She turned to find him standing in the doorway, his face pale with worry. "What are you doing? Put the book down." But it was too late. The book was no longer just a tool—it was a doorway. And the moment she touched it, she felt the door swing open, unleashing the full force of the entity that had haunted the shop for centuries. The energy crackled in the air, thick and tangible, twisting the very walls of the room.

Daniella's breath caught in her throat. She could feel the entity's presence pushing at her, invading her thoughts, her soul. She felt its hunger, its desire to break free of the cage she had helped create. It wanted out. And now, it was using her as a vessel.

"James!" she gasped, her voice strained as she dropped the book. But it was too late—the damage had been done.

The entity had returned.

James rushed to her side, his hands gripping her shoulders as he tried to steady her. But Daniella's eyes were wide with terror, her pulse racing. She could feel the darkness within her, stirring and shifting. It was no longer a separate force; it was a part of her, clawing at her insides, demanding to be set free.

"Daniella, look at me!" James pleaded, his voice frantic. "You have to fight it. You have to fight this."

"I can't," Daniella whispered, her voice trembling. "It's inside me. I—I thought I could control it, but it's too powerful. It's too strong."

The room seemed to close in around them. The walls warped and bent, the shelves groaning as though the very building was alive. Daniella could feel the power of the books reverberating through her, each one a conduit for the darkness. She was surrounded by it, suffocated by it. And the more she tried to fight, the more it took.

"James…" Daniella's voice was weak, strained. "I—I don't know how much longer I can hold on. I thought I could do this. I thought I could stop it. But I can't."

"No, Daniella," James insisted, his grip tightening on her arms. "You can. You have to."

But the darkness was already taking hold, and as Daniella looked into James's eyes, she saw the fear in his gaze. He was afraid of her. Of what she had become. And it shattered something deep inside her.

She tried to fight back. She focused on the part of her that was still her own—the part that had once been determined, brave. But the

1

entity within her was too strong, too overwhelming. It had consumed her completely, and there was no going back.

A voice, cold and guttural, whispered in her ear. You cannot stop it. You never could.

James stumbled backward, his face pale as he watched Daniella tremble, her hands shaking as the power inside her flared to life. Her body seemed to pulse with energy, her eyes flashing with an unnatural light. She was no longer just Daniella—the woman who had stepped into the shop all those weeks ago. She was something else, something dark and unrecognizable.

"Daniella…" James whispered, his voice barely audible. "Please." But it was no use. Daniella was lost. The books had taken her, and with her, the entity had been reborn. The darkness was free once again.

As Daniella stood there, her heart aching with the weight of her own loss, she realized that there was no more fight left. The entity was free. She had set it free. And now, all she could do was watch as the world she had known crumbled away into the very darkness she had tried so hard to keep at bay.

Chapter Six: THE UNRAVELING

"When everything falls apart, sometimes it's the breaking that makes us whole."

The world outside the bookshop had gone quiet, as if holding its breath in the wake of Daniella's transformation. The streets of Dublin, once bustling with the energy of holiday shoppers and festive cheer, were now eerily still. It was as if the darkness had spread, infecting not only the shop but the very air around them. Inside the shop, Daniella's transformation was complete. She stood at the center of the room, her body trembling with the power that surged within her, her eyes glowing an unnatural, almost alien shade of amber. The darkness she had tried so desperately to fight had consumed her—there was no longer any trace of the woman she had been.

James stood frozen, just outside her reach, his face pale and filled with a mixture of fear and disbelief. He had watched her struggle, had tried to save her, but now it was clear: Daniella was beyond saving. She had become the vessel for the very thing they had all feared.

"You're not yourself anymore," James said, his voice raw with emotion. "Daniella, please…"

Daniella's lips curled into a smile—one that was cold, empty, and far too knowing. She could feel the entity stirring inside her, feeding off her fear, her sorrow. It was powerful, more powerful than she could have ever imagined. And it wasn't just in her—it was spreading, reaching out like tendrils, infecting the very fabric of reality itself.

"You're right," Daniella said softly, her voice taking on a strange resonance, as if multiple voices were speaking through her. "I'm not myself. I never was."

The shop began to tremble, the shelves groaning under the pressure of the energy that crackled through the air. Daniella's eyes flicked toward the books, the ancient tomes that had been the source of all this. Their pages seemed to move of their own accord, whispering their dark secrets, beckoning her to open them, to unleash more of their power.

"You can't do this," James pleaded, taking a tentative step forward. "This isn't you. I know you're still in there, Daniella."

But Daniella's laughter echoed through the shop—dark, mocking, and empty.

"I am what the books made me," she replied, her voice chilling. "I am what the entity wanted. I am its key."

The books seemed to pulse in response to her words, their power growing stronger with each passing moment. The air in the shop was thick with the smell of old paper and something far darker—a presence that could no longer be ignored. Daniella could feel it, this ncient force within her, pushing her to do more, to give in to its demands.

"Stop it!" James shouted, his voice cracking with desperation. "You're not just destroying yourself, you're destroying everything around you!"

But Daniella barely registered his words. Her gaze was fixed on the books, the dark power calling to her, urging her to open them, to unleash their secrets.

A sudden crash broke through the tension in the air. The door to the shop slammed open with a force that rattled the windows, and Mr. Peters stepped inside, his face grim and determined. He had been in the back, organizing some of the more fragile books, but now he looked like a man who had come to a final decision.

"What have you done?" Mr. Peters asked, his voice low, filled with both anger and regret.

"I've opened the door," Daniella said, her voice echoing with an unnatural resonance. "I've set it free. The darkness is here now, Mr. Peters. It's not just in me anymore. It's in everything."

Mr. Peters took a slow, deliberate step toward her. "You're wrong. It's not in everything. It's in you. And if you don't stop, it will consume you completely."

"I want it to consume me," Daniella said, her smile widening. "I want to feel it. I want to become it."

James recoiled as he watched the scene unfold, his heart heavy with sorrow. Daniella wasn't just lost to the darkness—she was embracing it. She had become the very thing they had feared. He had failed her.

But he couldn't let her fall any further. He had to try.

"You're stronger than this," he said, his voice pleading.

"Don't let it take you. I know the real you is still in there. Fight it, Daniella. Please, fight for yourself."

For a brief moment, Daniella's expression flickered. There was something in her eyes, something like recognition, but it was gone as quickly as it came. The entity had a hold on her now.

"I am the real me," Daniella responded, her voice cold and final. "And the real me has accepted what I am."

Before either James or Mr. Peters could react, the shop seemed to shift. The lights flickered, casting eerie shadows across the room. The walls seemed to pulse with an unnatural energy, and the books began to shift on their own, their pages turning in a rush of wind. The darkness, once sealed away, had found its way back into the world—and now, it was closer than ever.

The shop trembled once again as Daniella reached out toward the nearest book, her hand shaking as she touched its spine. She felt a surge of power, and the entity stirred within her, delighted by the contact.

James stepped forward, his voice filled with determination.

"Daniella, please! Don't do it!"

But Daniella's eyes were blank, her expression empty. She was lost—lost to the books, lost to the entity that had claimed her as its own.

And just as her fingers brushed the cover of the book, ready to open it and unlock the full force of the darkness, a surge of power erupted from the pages. Daniella screamed, but it wasn't her voice that filled the room. It was the voice of the entity—loud, triumphant, and filled with malice. The ground beneath them cracked, and the shop seemed to split open, the walls collapsing in on themselves as the darkness erupted, consuming everything in its path. The books flew from their shelves, swirling in the air like a storm, their pages glowing with an unnatural light.

James reached for Daniella, but it was too late. She had become one with the darkness.

And with that, the world around them began to unravel.

The world around Daniella was unraveling, a storm of chaos unleashed by the books, the entity, and her own choices. The shop, once a quaint and peaceful haven of ink and paper, had transformed into a swirling vortex of darkness and power. The walls groaned as they cracked and shifted, and the once familiar shelves of books now twisted like living creatures, reaching out with the same hunger that had overtaken her.

Daniella stood at the heart of it all, her body shaking as the entity pulsed within her, an insatiable hunger growing with every passing second. She could feel its power coursing through her veins, every part of her consumed by its presence. It was no longer just a voice in her head—it was her, and she was it. She had become the very thing she had once feared.

James stood frozen at the door, his eyes wide with horror. The shop was collapsing around him, the energy in the room growing more erratic and dangerous by the second. The books, once harmless relics of the past, now seemed to have a life of their own, their pages fluttering in the air like wings of some ancient beast. The floor trembled beneath his feet, and the air itself seemed thick with power.

"Daniella!" he shouted, his voice trembling with desperation. "This isn't you! This isn't what you wanted!"

But Daniella's eyes—those amber eyes—were vacant, filled only with the cold, dark presence of the entity. She turned slowly toward him, a twisted smile playing across her lips.

"It's too late, James," she said softly, her voice a mix of her own and something darker. "You can't save me now. You never could."

Mr. Peters, who had been silently watching the chaos unfold, finally stepped forward, his face grim with determination. He had known that this day would come, but seeing it in front of him—seeing Daniella so fully lost to the darkness—was harder than he had ever anticipated.

"We can still fight this," Mr. Peters said, his voice firm despite the tremor in the air. "Daniella, listen to me. There is still a way out. You're stronger than this. You can push it out."

But Daniella only laughed, the sound like nails scraping across a chalkboard.

"No," she replied, her voice cold and final. "I'm exactly where I need to be. We are exactly where we need to be."

The entity within Daniella stirred, its voice rippling through her thoughts, twisting her sense of self. Yes, Daniella. You were always meant for this. You were meant to lead us to freedom. Together, we will reshape everything.

Her body trembled as the power surged within her, and the books began to move of their own accord, their pages glowing brightly with dark energy. The shop seemed to breathe, the walls expanding and contracting with the force of the entity's power.

James stepped forward, his heart pounding in his chest. He couldn't let her go. He couldn't let the woman he had once known be consumed by this darkness.

"Daniella, listen to me!" James cried, his voice desperate. "I know you're still in there. You're still you. You can fight this! Please, for all of us, fight it."

But Daniella's eyes flickered, the faintest trace of doubt appearing in the depths of her gaze. For a moment, the entity faltered, as if unsure of itself. James seized the opportunity, his voice filled with urgency.

"You are not alone in this," he said, his words steady and filled with conviction. "I won't leave you. We can fight together, Daniella. We can fix this."

For a brief moment, Daniella's expression softened, a flicker of the woman she used to be breaking through the dark veil of the entity's influence. Her breath came in short, ragged gasps as she fought to regain control.

And then, just as quickly as it had appeared, the flicker vanished. The entity inside her surged with renewed power, and Daniella's

69

body shuddered violently. The air around them crackled with energy, and the ground beneath their feet began to shake.

"No!" she screamed, her voice a mixture of her own and the entity's. "I am not yours to save!"

The shop's destruction accelerated as the darkness wrapped itself around Daniella, twisting and reshaping her until she was no longer just a woman. She was a conduit for the entity's full power. The books, now vibrating with the force of the entity, swirled in the air, their pages glowing with an eerie, unholy light.

Mr. Peters stepped back, his face grave. "It's too strong now," he whispered. "The only way to stop it… is to close the door. But it requires a sacrifice."

James looked at him, panic flooding his veins. "What do you mean?"

"The books," Mr. Peters continued, his voice heavy with regret. "They can be sealed away, but it requires the soul of the one who opened the door. Daniella must be the one to close it. She is the key."

Daniella's gaze locked onto James, her eyes burning with an intensity that made his heart race. "You were always weak," she said, her voice a cruel mockery of the woman he had known. "You couldn't stop me. No one could."

"You don't have to do this, Daniella," James said, his voice low, full of anguish. "You're not this. You're not this thing."

But Daniella only smiled, a hollow, twisted thing. "The real question, James, is whether you're willing to pay the price to stop me."

With a final, earth-shattering roar, the books exploded in a burst of light, the shop collapsing in on itself as the darkness swarmed toward Daniella. The very foundations of reality seemed to shudder, and everything—everything—was at the brink of total destruction.

James couldn't look away. The woman he had tried to save was lost. But there was one last chance, one final effort.

He grabbed the nearest book, opened it to its first page, and in a voice filled with determination, he began to read.

The room spun as the words poured from his mouth, ancient incantations woven into the fabric of the universe itself. The books trembled, their pages turning wildly as the power of the entity fought back against the incantation. Daniella screamed, her body convulsing as the darkness inside her fought to break free.

But James's voice grew stronger. This is the end.

The entity screamed, its voice filled with rage as the words of the spell began to close the door. Daniella's body jerked violently, her eyes widening with horror as the force of the power struck her. The books, the darkness—they were being sealed away once again.

And then, with one final, anguished cry, Daniella collapsed to the ground.

The darkness lingered, its heavy presence still hanging in the air as Daniella lay motionless on the floor of the wrecked bookshop. The once-thriving shop was now a hollow shell, its walls cracked and crumbling as the last remnants of the malevolent force dissipated. The eerie glow from the books had faded, leaving nothing but shadows and silence in its wake.

James stood over Daniella, his heart pounding in his chest. The entity, the books, the dark power that had consumed her—had it truly all been sealed away? He couldn't be sure. The price had been steep, but it wasn't over yet. The world around him had been fractured, torn apart by the battle for Daniella's soul. And now, standing amidst the ruins of the bookshop, he couldn't shake the feeling that there was more to this ending than it seemed.

Daniella stirred, a soft groan escaping her lips. Her body was heavy, as if the weight of the darkness that had taken root inside her had drained the very life from her bones. Her eyes fluttered open, blinking against the dim light.

"James?" she whispered, her voice hoarse and unsteady.

James dropped to his knees beside her, taking her hand in his.

"Daniella," he breathed, his voice thick with emotion. "You're back. You're you again."

She turned her head toward him, her eyes clouded with confusion. For a moment, she didn't seem to remember what had happened, the events that had led her to this point. It was as if she had been asleep, lost in a dream she couldn't quite grasp.

But then, as the fog lifted from her mind, her eyes widened with realization. "The books," she whispered, her voice tinged with horror. "I… I opened it. I let it in…"

She sat up slowly, her face pale, and her breath quickened. "It was never supposed to go this far. I… I lost myself."

James placed a hand on her shoulder, his gaze soft but firm. "You fought, Daniella. You fought harder than anyone could have. And now, it's over. The darkness is gone."

But Daniella wasn't so sure. There was a weight in her chest, a gnawing feeling that something was still wrong. She could feel the faintest pulse, like a heartbeat deep within her, a reminder of the entity's presence. The books had been sealed away, the door closed, but part of her—the darkest part—still remained. It was a constant reminder of what had happened, and what could happen again.

"The door is closed," she said quietly, as if to reassure herself. "But it still feels like something is inside me… like it's waiting."

James frowned, his hand still resting on her shoulder. "We can't go back, Daniella. We have to look forward now. This is the moment we start over."

But just as he spoke those words, a chilling sound echoed through the wreckage of the shop—a low, rumbling growl that sent a shiver down their spines. The air seemed to pulse with malevolent energy, and the faintest flicker of light danced from the pages of the remaining books scattered across the floor. They hadn't all been destroyed. Some still remained, untouched by the spell.

The sound grew louder, more distinct, as if something—someone— was trying to break free from the pages.

"No," Daniella whispered, her voice trembling. "It can't be. It's still here…"

73

Before either of them could react, a figure emerged from the shadows, a shape rising from the wreckage of the bookshelves. It was tall and imposing, its form a blur of shifting darkness. The figure stepped forward, its face obscured by the shadows, but the energy it radiated was unmistakable.

James reached for the nearest object—a fallen book—but it was too late. The figure's eyes gleamed with a dangerous light, and its voice rang out, deep and resonant, echoing through the space.

"Foolish," the voice hissed. "You thought you had destroyed me. But the darkness is eternal. It cannot be contained."

The figure advanced, and as it did, the shadows around it seemed to warp and twist, pulling at the very fabric of reality. Daniella stood, her body trembling as she faced the figure. This was the true price— the price of salvation. The darkness was never truly gone; it had merely been waiting for the right moment to return.

And it had returned, more powerful than ever.

"You sealed the door," the figure said, its voice dripping with malice. "But you are the key to unlocking it once more."

Daniella's heart sank as the realization hit her. She was the conduit—the only one who could hold the darkness back. And with her faltering strength, the entity had returned, its power clawing at her, ready to take control once more.

James stepped forward, his hand gripping Daniella's tightly. "We won't let you win," he declared, his voice steady despite the fear that threatened to consume him. "We will fight. We've already fought once. And we'll fight again."

The figure laughed, its voice like the sound of thunder. "You cannot fight what is already inside you."

Daniella's body convulsed, her breath shallow and labored as the entity's power surged through her. She could feel it—the darkness, whispering in her mind, promising freedom, power, everything she had ever desired. But she also felt the love, the warmth of the people who had fought for her, who had saved her.

"James…" she whispered, her voice barely audible. "I don't want to become this again."

"You won't," he replied firmly, pulling her close. "I won't let you." With those words, Daniella made a decision—a choice that would determine her fate. She closed her eyes, pushing against the pull of the darkness, gathering the strength she had left. She could feel the battle raging inside her—the entity clawing at her mind, trying to drag her back into its grip. But she wouldn't let it win. Not again. A surge of power erupted from Daniella, a flash of pure light that pushed back the figure, forcing it to retreat into the shadows. The books, still scattered across the floor, began to tremble and writhe, their pages flicking like the wings of trapped birds. The air hummed with energy, and Daniella stood tall, her hand still clasped tightly in James's.

She had chosen the light. And with that choice, she sealed the darkness once more.

As the entity vanished, retreating into the void, the bookshop began to settle. The walls stopped shaking, the air cleared, and the books slowly returned to their shelves, as if nothing had ever happened.

But Daniella knew that this victory was only temporary. The darkness would always be waiting, lurking in the shadows. But for now, she had won. And she had found something she never thought possible: peace.

Chapter Seven: THE BROKEN BRIDGE

"Sometimes, to rebuild what was broken, we must first confront the pieces we left behind."

The bookshop was silent now, its once-chaotic energy dissipating into a quiet that was almost eerie. Daniella stood at the center of it all, her breath steady, but her mind was a whirlwind. Her victory had been hard-won, but the price was still fresh, like a scar she couldn't ignore. The darkness had been repelled, yes, but the battle had left its mark—not just on the shop or on her, but on the relationships she had taken for granted.

James stood beside her, his hand still gripping hers, but the weight between them was heavier now. There was a kind of distance between them, a gap that had widened during the course of this ordeal. He had fought for her, and she had fought for herself. But now, standing in the aftermath, Daniella couldn't help but wonder if their fight had only made the gap harder to bridge.

"I never wanted to hurt you, James," Daniella said, her voice soft, almost tentative. She didn't dare look at him, afraid that if she did, she would crumble beneath the weight of his gaze.

James let out a sigh, his fingers tightening around hers, but not with the desperation he had once felt. Instead, there was a quiet understanding. "I know. But the question is, Daniella, did you ever truly see me? Or was I just someone to fight for while you fought yourself?"

Her chest tightened at the truth of his words. Had she really seen him? Or had she been so caught up in her own struggles, her own darkness that she hadn't even noticed the quiet sacrifices he had made for her? The realization hit her like a wave, drowning her in guilt. James had always been there, but had she truly been there for him?

The silence between them stretched, thick and painful. Daniella couldn't shake the feeling that no matter how much they tried to rebuild, there was something permanently fractured in the foundation of their relationship. Maybe it was the things unsaid, the guilt, or the distance that had grown between them during their time in the bookshop. Or maybe it was just that they were both different people now—shaped by the darkness, and forever marked by the things they had seen and endured.

"We've both changed," Daniella murmured, her eyes finally meeting his. "We've been through things that no one should ever have to go through, and maybe that's just… something we can't come back from. Maybe we were never meant to be the way we were before."

James met her gaze, his expression soft, but his eyes distant.

"Maybe. But that doesn't mean we can't find a new way to be— together or apart."

The words hung in the air, and Daniella's heart sank. She hadn't been ready for this—hadn't expected this conversation to come so oon, so suddenly. She had thought that, once the darkness was gone, everything would go back to normal. But the truth was, there was no going back. There was only moving forward, and neither of them knew what that would look like.

Before either of them could say more, the door to the bookshop creaked open, the sound cutting through the stillness. They turned to see Mr. Peters standing in the doorway, his face as grave as ever.

"I didn't want to interrupt," he said quietly, his voice low. "But here's something you need to see."

Daniella exchanged a look with James before walking toward the door. Her mind was still a tangle of confusion, but curiosity gnawed at her. What could Mr. Peters possibly have to show them now? Had the darkness truly been sealed away, or was something else waiting?

Mr. Peters led them down the narrow, crumbling corridor of the bookshop, his footsteps echoing in the silence. He stopped in front of a door they had never noticed before, a door that seemed to appear out of nowhere. It was old, its wood worn and faded, and it creaked as Mr. Peters pushed it open.

Behind the door was a room Daniella had never seen—hidden in the depths of the bookshop, a secret that had been concealed for as long as the shop had stood.

Inside, the room was filled with books, but not the kind of books they were used to. These books were ancient, their covers dusted with centuries of neglect. They seemed to hum with an energy that made the hairs on the back of Daniella's neck stand on end.

"What's this?" Daniella whispered, stepping into the room. She reached for one of the books, but Mr. Peters stopped her.

"Those books," he said, his voice trembling slightly, "are the true power of the shop. They were here long before you ever walked through that door. And now… now they are the final test."

Daniella looked at him, confusion etching her face. "Test? What test?"

Mr. Peters hesitated, then stepped forward, his eyes filled with a mixture of regret and fear. "You see, Daniella, the entity you faced was never the only one. The darkness that was inside you—it was just one fragment of a much larger force. And these books… these books hold the true power to either bind it forever or unleash it once more."

Daniella's heart pounded in her chest as she absorbed the weight of his words. This wasn't over. She hadn't sealed the darkness away—she had only contained a fragment of it. And now, the true battle was just beginning.

"The books?" Daniella asked, her voice barely a whisper. "What do I have to do with them?"

Mr. Peters looked at her, his face drawn and weary. "They are connected to you, Daniella. You were chosen. And you must decide: do you risk it all to try and stop what is still out there… or do you walk away and leave it to fester?"

The room seemed to close in around her, the weight of the decision pressing down on her shoulders. She had thought the fight was over.

But now, she realized with a sickening clarity, that it had only just begun.

Daniella stood motionless, staring at the ancient books in front of her. The air seemed to thrum with an unseen energy, vibrating with the power that lay within the room. She had faced the darkness. She had sealed it away. But now, standing before these ancient tomes, she realized she was being asked to make a choice that could change everything.

"Why me?" Daniella's voice cracked, the weight of her uncertainty pressing down on her. She had spent so long fighting the shadows within her, trying to escape the past that she couldn't fathom why she was being dragged back into this war. "Why now? Why these books?"

Mr. Peters' gaze softened, and for the first time, she saw the depth of the burden he carried. He stepped closer to her, his face etched with the sorrow of someone who had witnessed too many tragedies. "You were always meant to be a part of this," he said quietly, almost regretfully. "These books—they have a purpose. A purpose that's tied to you. The entity that you fought—it wasn't the beginning, nor will it be the end. You've kept it at bay, but you're connected to the force that birthed it."

Daniella's breath hitched. "I don't understand. You're saying I'm part of this... this curse?"

Mr. Peters nodded slowly. "In a way. The darkness that plagued you was born from the pages of these books. It was fed by the same power that pulses through them. And it's waiting—waiting for the one who holds the key."

James stepped forward, his voice full of concern. "What do you mean, Daniella holds the key? Are you saying she's part of the reason this curse exists?"

Mr. Peters hesitated before answering, as though the truth was too dangerous to utter. "The books are not mere objects. They were created to guard a power, an ancient and terrible force. Over time, they became corrupted, their purpose twisted, until they became instruments of darkness. Daniella's blood—her connection to the legacy of this place—was the catalyst that brought it all back."

Daniella's mind reeled. She couldn't comprehend what she was hearing. She had always felt like an outsider, like something was missing in her life. But this? This was beyond anything she could have imagined.

"So… what am I supposed to do?" she whispered, her voice trembling. "You're telling me that I'm the one who can stop it? Or unleash it?"

Mr. Peters looked her in the eye, his expression hard. "You're the keeper now, Daniella. And you must choose. Do you seal the power away once and for all? Or do you risk everything to use it—control it—and perhaps, just maybe, stop what's coming?"

The room grew colder, the air thickening with a palpable sense of doom. Daniella felt her pulse quicken. It was as if the very books themselves were calling to her, urging her to make a choice. A choice she wasn't sure she was ready to make.

"The power inside these books…" Daniella started, her voice barely above a whisper, "Is it the same power that controlled me? The one that… made me do things I couldn't control?"

"Yes," Mr. Peters replied. "The same power. It's what you fought in yourself. And now it's waiting for you to make a decision. But be warned—once the choice is made, there is no going back."

Daniella's eyes scanned the room. The books stood there, silent and waiting, their leather-bound covers glowing faintly. She could feel their pull. And she could feel the weight of the decision pressing against her, like a storm on the horizon that she couldn't avoid.

"I can't do this," Daniella muttered, shaking her head. "I'm not strong enough."

James stepped closer, his hand resting gently on her shoulder.

"Daniella, you've already done the impossible. You fought that darkness and won. You can do this too."

She turned to look at him, her eyes full of doubt. "But what if I fail? What if I become it?"

James smiled softly, a mixture of affection and confidence in his expression. "You won't. You're not alone in this. You've got me. You've got yourself. And you've got the strength to make the right choice."

The words settled in her mind like a seed, planting a small spark of hope amidst the uncertainty. Could she really do this? Could she choose to seal the power away and prevent the catastrophe she could feel looming over them all?

Her gaze returned to the books. She could feel the darkness thrumming beneath their covers, calling to her like a siren's song. But alongside that darkness was something else—something warm, something human. It was the same thing she had felt when she looked at James, when she thought about the people who had fought for her. It was hope. And it was stronger than any darkness she had ever known.

Daniella took a deep breath, her heart racing as she made her decision. She reached out, her fingers brushing the cover of the nearest book. It was an electric touch, the energy from the book surging through her, but she held firm.

"I will stop it," she said, her voice steady. "I will seal it. Forever."

Mr. Peters' face softened with relief, but his eyes also held a deep sadness. "You don't know what you're sacrificing, Daniella."

"I don't care," she replied. "I don't care what it costs. It's the only way to keep everyone safe."

With those words, she pulled the book from its place on the shelf. The moment her fingers gripped the cover, the room seemed to shake, the air thickening as the very foundation of the shop seemed to groan in protest. The power surged, testing her resolve, but Daniella fought back. She had faced the darkness once before. She could do it again.

The pages of the book began to turn on their own, as if the very act of opening it was enough to unlock the ancient power contained within. Daniella's hands shook as she read the text—an incantation, a spell, a ritual that could either save them all or destroy everything she had ever known.

With a deep breath, she recited the words aloud, her voice unwavering as she called upon the ancient magic to seal the darkness away for good. The air around her crackled with energy, and for a moment, it felt as though the world itself was holding its breath.

The final word left her lips, and the room fell deathly silent. The power in the book was gone, sealed away, leaving Daniella with nothing but the quiet hum of her own heartbeat.

But the cost of that decision wasn't yet clear. The darkness had been sealed—but at what price?

Chapter Eight: THE ECHO OF CHOICES

"In the silence after a choice, the echoes of what could have been are often louder than the decision itself."

Daniella stood in the center of the room, the ancient book still clasped tightly in her hands, its power now dormant. The air was heavy with the tension of the moment, and the stillness was almost suffocating. The bookshelves, once alive with a dark hum, were now quiet. The shadows no longer seemed to watch her with hungry eyes. But the silence wasn't comforting. It felt like the calm before the storm.

James stood beside her, his face pale, his expression unreadable. He had watched her recite the incantation, his hand gripping her shoulder in solidarity, but now he looked as though he was holding his breath—waiting for something, anything, to happen.

"Is it over?" he asked, his voice barely above a whisper. He didn't want to ask, didn't want to break the fragile peace that had settled in the room, but the question was there, and it couldn't be ignored.

Daniella didn't answer right away. She stood there, staring at the book in her hands, feeling its presence. It was no longer pulsing with power, but the weight of what she had just done felt heavier than anything she had ever carried. She had sealed away the darkness, but she hadn't vanquished it.

No, the darkness wasn't gone. It had only been pushed back into the corners of the world. And there was always the possibility it could return.

"I think… I think it's over for now," Daniella said at last, her voice distant. "But it's not gone forever, James. I can feel it. It's still out there, waiting."

James nodded grimly, his eyes still filled with concern. "So what do we do now?"

Daniella hesitated. The question seemed so simple, but the answer was anything but. How could she go back to a normal life when everything had changed so dramatically? She had made her choice, but that didn't erase the cost of it. Her blood was tied to this curse. And even now, she could feel the ripples of her decision spreading outward, as though she had opened a door that couldn't be shut again.

"We keep moving forward," she finally said, her voice quiet but resolute. "We have to."

The sound of footsteps echoed through the bookshop, and both Daniella and James turned toward the doorway. Mr. Peters stood there, his face grim but not unkind. He didn't speak at first, merely observing them, as though waiting to see what they would do next.

"The shop is safe now," he said, his voice like gravel, "but the question remains. What happens to the keeper after the power is gone?"

Daniella swallowed hard. Mr. Peters's words struck a chord in her. She hadn't thought about that—the keeper. What happened to someone who had borne the weight of such power? Was she forever bound to the choices she had made, forever marked by the darkness she had confronted?

"I don't know," she said softly, her eyes dropping to the floor. "But I'll find out."

They all stood in the doorway, the weight of the moment still heavy between them. It felt as though time had stopped, as though the world outside the bookshop had paused, waiting for their next move. And for the first time in what felt like ages, Daniella realized something—the world had never stopped moving.

The events in the bookshop were just a ripple in a much larger tide. The darkness was part of something bigger. She hadn't just sealed away an evil force; she had stepped into something ancient, something greater than her own fears. And now she had to face that something head-on.

James's hand found hers, his grip tight. "You're not alone in this," he whispered.

Daniella looked up at him, her eyes full of gratitude and guilt. "I don't deserve you," she murmured, her voice breaking. "I don't deserve any of this."

"Yes, you do," he said firmly. "You've fought for it. You've fought for yourself. You deserve peace, Daniella."

Her chest tightened at his words. She wanted to believe him. She wanted to believe that after all this—after the shadows, the books, the choices—she could find peace. But the road ahead wasn't clear, and she knew it. The world hadn't stopped. It never did. And while she had sealed the darkness away for now, there would always be another battle. Another moment when the past would come knocking, demanding more of her than she was willing to give.

Mr. Peters's voice cut through her thoughts. "There's one more thing you should know, Daniella," he said, his tone serious.

She turned to him, her brow furrowed. "What is it?"

He stepped closer, his eyes meeting hers. "The darkness you faced... it wasn't just born of the books. It was born of something much older, much more powerful. And it won't rest. It will wait until the next keeper is chosen."

Her heart skipped a beat. "The next keeper? What do you mean?"

Mr. Peters hesitated, as if considering how much to reveal. "The curse doesn't end with you, Daniella. You've sealed it for now, but the books—they're not done yet. One day, they will choose another keeper. And when that time comes, they will look to someone who is willing to bear the burden."

Daniella felt her blood run cold. The books weren't finished with her. The power she had just sealed away would not fade. It would wait. And it would choose again.

As the weight of Mr. Peters's words settled into her chest, Daniella realized one undeniable truth: she could never truly escape what she had become. The keeper. The one who had fought the darkness—and might have to again.

And as the world outside the bookshop slowly began to stir, she knew that her life, her very existence, would never be the same.

The chill in the bookshop seemed to deepen, a sudden cold creeping beneath Daniella's skin as she stood there, the weight of Mr. Peters' words pressing down on her. The idea that this battle, the one she thought she had won, could be far from over sent a tremor through her body. She had sealed the darkness away, but in truth, she had only delayed its return. The books hadn't been destroyed. The curse hadn't been broken. It had simply been paused.

The very thought of it made her want to run, to escape. But she couldn't. Not anymore. She was the keeper, bound to this fate whether she accepted it or not.

James stood next to her, his gaze searching her face. He must have sensed the sudden shift in her energy, the way her body had tensed, the weight of an unseen burden settling onto her shoulders.

"What is it?" he asked softly, his voice filled with concern.

Daniella's eyes met his, and for a moment, she couldn't speak. She wanted to tell him everything, to share the fear that had now taken root inside her. But the words stuck in her throat, the reality of the situation too much to process in the silence of the moment.

"The curse…" she began slowly, her voice trembling despite her efforts to sound steady. "It's not over, James. It won't be until the books are destroyed. And we both know that can never happen."

Mr. Peters stepped forward, his face hardening with an expression of resolve. "Daniella's right. The curse was never meant to be permanent. The books were always meant to be kept, watched over. They contain far too much power. Too much darkness."

"What do you mean by 'watched over'?" James demanded, his voice rising. "You said the books were sealed. If they're so dangerous, why are they still here?"

"They were sealed, yes," Mr. Peters replied, his voice grave. "But sealing them doesn't erase their power. It simply locks it away. The force that resides in those pages is older than any of us. And it's not easily contained."

The room seemed to grow colder still, the air thick with the oppressive weight of the truth. Daniella's breath came in shallow bursts as she tried to steady herself. The darkness was still out there, and sooner or later, it would find a way to return. The books would call to it, just as they had called to her. They would call to someone else—someone who would be foolish or desperate enough to unlock the pages.

But what terrified her more than the thought of the curse returning was the thought of losing control. She had fought so hard to regain her sense of self. She couldn't let herself fall back into the grip of that power, not again.

"Is there no way to truly destroy them?" Daniella asked, her voice low, filled with disbelief.

Mr. Peters shook his head. "They're indestructible. The power they hold is ancient, too deeply woven into the fabric of this world. The only way to truly rid ourselves of them is to…" He trailed off, as if the next words were too dangerous to say.

"To what?" Daniella urged, stepping closer, desperate for answers.

"To destroy the keeper," Mr. Peters whispered.

The words hung in the air like a death sentence. Daniella felt her chest tighten, the world suddenly spinning around her. She had always known the danger of becoming the keeper, but this? This was something she hadn't anticipated.

She took a step back, her hands trembling. "You mean to say… if I want to end this curse, I have to die?"

Mr. Peters nodded, his face filled with sorrow. "The keeper's blood is tied to the curse. If you die, the curse dies with you."

Daniella staggered back, her mind reeling from the weight of what he was saying. She had spent so much time fighting to stay alive, to protect herself and those around her. But now, she was faced with a terrible truth. The very thing that had brought her power—the very thing that had made her strong—was also the thing that would keep this curse alive.

"I can't," she whispered, her voice breaking. "I can't die. I've worked so hard for this life. I won't just… give it up."

James stepped forward, his hand finding hers, his grip firm and unwavering. "You don't have to. We'll find another way. There's always another way."

Daniella shook her head, her heart heavy with the weight of her responsibilities. "No, James. There isn't. If we don't do this, the curse will keep coming back. And I'll be trapped in this never-ending cycle of death and darkness. We can't escape it. Not unless I—"

"No!" James interrupted, his voice rising in desperation. "We're not doing this. There has to be another way. I won't lose you. I won't let you sacrifice yourself."

Tears filled Daniella's eyes, and for the first time in what felt like an eternity, she allowed herself to break. She leaned into James, seeking comfort in his presence. "I don't want to die," she whispered, her voice thick with emotion. "I don't want to be the keeper anymore. But if I don't stop this, if I don't finish what I started, it will never end."

James pulled her close, his arms wrapping around her protectively. "We'll find a way," he promised, his voice filled with determination. "I don't care what it takes. We'll fight this together."

But in the back of Daniella's mind, a voice echoed—cold, distant, and all too familiar. The darkness was coming. It was patient, waiting, as it always had. And no matter how much she wished for another path, she knew in her heart that there was no escaping the consequences of her choices.

The keeper's fate had always been sealed.

As the night wore on, the tension in the air seemed to grow thicker. Outside, the winds began to howl, and the streets of Dublin became eerily quiet. Inside the bookshop, Daniella, James, and Mr. Peters stood together, knowing that their fight was far from over. The darkness would return. And when it did, the keeper would have to make a choice.

The night seemed endless, stretching before Daniella like an ocean of darkness. The air inside the bookshop had grown colder, heavier, as though the walls themselves were pressing in on her. She could feel it—the weight of the curse, the pressure of the decision that lay before her. The shadow of her own fate hung over her like a guillotine, and no matter how hard she tried to escape it, it remained. James was at her side, his presence a silent comfort. He had promised they would find a way, but Daniella knew deep down that no amount of love or determination would change the truth. The curse had been set in motion long before she had ever come to this place. And no matter how she fought, it would claim its price.

The only question was—would she pay it willingly?

Mr. Peters stood across from them, his eyes hollow with the knowledge he had imparted. His face was grim, worn with years of carrying the burden of being the keeper. He had watched others fall to the darkness, had seen them make the same choices Daniella now faced.

"There's no easy way out, Daniella," he said softly. "The curse has always required a price. It's not just about death—it's about sacrifice. The keeper is bound to the power, to the books. There's no walking away from it without a cost."

"I know," Daniella whispered, her voice trembling. "But I can't die. Not like this. Not when there's still so much left to fight for."

James reached out, taking her hand gently in his. "Then we'll find another way. We have to. You're not doing this alone."

Daniella's heart twisted at his words. She wanted so desperately to believe him, to believe that there could be another way. But as the moments passed, a cold realization settled over her—the curse was ancient. It had survived centuries. She was just a pawn in a much larger game. Her fate had been written long before she had ever stepped into this bookshop.

The door to the back room creaked open, and Daniella turned, her heart pounding in her chest. A figure stood in the doorway—tall, cloaked in shadows. The air seemed to shift around him, the temperature dropping several degrees as if the very essence of the darkness had arrived.

It was him. The author. The one who had sought out the power of the books. His eyes glinted with something cold and predatory, a smile curling on his lips as he took a step forward.

"You've done well, Daniella," he said, his voice smooth and dark, like velvet. "But it's time for the next chapter."

Daniella's breath caught in her throat. The man who had appeared out of nowhere—who had been nothing but a distant figure in the periphery of her life—was now here, standing before her. She hadn't expected him to show up, but she had known, somewhere deep inside, that he would.

The author, the one who had been pulling the strings from the shadows. The one who had been feeding the curse all along.

"Why?" she asked, her voice barely audible. "Why have you done this? All of this? Was it just to use the books? To feed your own power?"

He chuckled, a sound that sent chills down her spine. "Oh, it's much more than that, my dear. The books are just a means to an end. The power contained within them is limitless, and I plan to harness it all.

95

You, Daniella, were just a stepping stone. The keeper's blood, the curse, they're all part of a larger design. You were never meant to escape."

James stepped forward, his face flushed with anger. "No one is using her. Not anymore."

The author's eyes shifted to James, studying him with mild amusement. "You think you can stop this? You're too late. The curse has already begun. There's no undoing it now."

Daniella felt the familiar pulse of dark energy begin to stir in the room. It was subtle at first, just a shift in the air, but it grew, swelling like a storm. She could feel it, could sense it wrapping itself around her. The power was calling her, tempting her to give in. She could feel her blood heating, the hunger for control whispering in her ear.

She closed her eyes, struggling to fight it. But the power was stronger than ever before, pulling at her, urging her to accept it. To give in.

"You don't have to do this," James said, his voice raw with desperation. "I won't let you become what he wants you to be."

Daniella opened her eyes, her heart breaking at the sight of him. He was willing to fight for her, to risk everything to keep her safe. But the darkness… it was too much. She could feel it creeping in, threatening to take control of her once again.

The author stepped closer, his presence like a weight on her chest. "You can't escape it, Daniella. You are the keeper. It's in your blood. All I have to do is take what's mine."

And in that moment, the choice was clear.

Daniella's mind raced as the power began to surge through her. She could feel the books calling to her, the shadows reaching out, begging her to give in. The temptation was unbearable. It was everything she had fought against, everything she had feared.

But she could not—she would not—let herself become the thing she feared most.

With every ounce of strength she could muster, Daniella took a step back from the author, from the darkness, from the curse. "No," she whispered, her voice shaking. "I won't let you win. I'll fight. I'll fight until the end."

And just like that, with a single, decisive act of will, Daniella broke free from the darkness. She turned away from the books, from the shadows, and in a moment of clarity, she did the one thing that would end it all—she closed the door to the bookshop, locking the curse inside.

The author's face twisted in fury as the curse began to recede, the darkness retreating into the void from which it had come. The power of the books began to fade, their grip loosening, and for the first time in years, the air in the bookshop felt light again.

Daniella turned to James, her eyes filled with tears. She had done it. She had chosen to live. And in doing so, she had taken back her life, her freedom.

"We're free," she whispered, her voice barely audible.

And as they stood together, the storm outside finally began to subside, the wind dying down, and the darkness that had once ruled their lives faded into nothing.

The curse was broken.

The keeper was free.

EPILOGUE

"Sometimes, to find freedom, you must first lose yourself in the shadows."

Months had passed since the night Daniella faced the curse and won. The bookshop now stood quiet, its shelves orderly, and the lingering darkness banished to the forgotten corners where no human hand would venture. Outside, spring had begun to stretch its warm fingers across Dublin, melting the last of winter's frost.

Daniella stood in the doorway, holding a cup of steaming tea, watching the morning sunlight stream through the windows. The shop looked different now—less like a prison and more like a sanctuary. She had taken the first steps to reclaim her life, pouring her energy into restoring the shop's charm. It was no longer a trap but a place of wonder and discovery.

James had left, as he said he would. Yet, his promise lingered: that he would return, perhaps one day when the wounds had healed and the ghosts had faded. Daniella missed him, but she also knew she wasn't the same woman she had been before. She didn't need saving anymore.

A gentle knock at the door startled her. She turned to see Maria standing there, a hesitant smile on her face, holding a small wrapped gift.

"Thought I'd drop by," Maria said. "To see how you're doing."

Daniella smiled, her heart lighter than it had been in years. "Come in," she said, stepping aside.

As Maria entered, the bell above the door chimed—a sound that no longer sent shivers down Daniella's spine. For the first time, it was just a bell, welcoming someone into the shop.

The curse was gone. The secrets had been laid to rest. And in their place, Daniella had found something unexpected: a chance to rebuild, to forgive, and to begin again.

Somewhere on the highest shelf, one book remained sealed, its cover blank, its story yet unwritten. Daniella glanced at it briefly before turning her attention back to her sister. She would leave it there, undisturbed—a reminder of the past, and of the future she had chosen to reclaim.

For the first time in years, Daniella felt ready. Whatever came next, she would face it on her own terms. And as the sun rose higher, bathing the bookshop in golden light, she knew this was only the beginning.

www.ingramcontent.com/pod-product-compliance
Lightning Source LLC
Chambersburg PA
CBHW050813250726
48653CB00006B/2200